THE SALINAS VALLEY

Jennie Verardo

Denzil Verardo

"Partners in Progress" by John Waters

Produced in cooperation with
the Salinas Chamber of Commerce

Windsor Publications, Inc.
Chatsworth, California

THE SALINAS VALLEY

AN ILLUSTRATED HISTORY

By Jennie Dennis Verardo and Denzil Verardo

Windsor Publications, Inc.—History Books Division
Managing Editor: Karen Story
Design Director: Alexander D'Anca

Staff for *The Salinas Valley: An Illustrated History*
Manuscript Editor: Kevin Taylor
Photo Editor: Loren Prostano
Editor, Corporate Biographies: Brenda Berryhill
Production Editor, Corporate Biographies: Albert J. Polito
Proofreader: Douglas P. Lathrop
Editorial Assistants: Kim Kievman, Michael Nugwynne, Kathy B. Peyser,
   Priscilla Solis, Theresa J. Solis
Publisher's Representative, Corporate Biographies: Gina Woolf
Layout Artist: Thomas McTighe
Layout Artist, Corporate Biographies: Mari Catherine Preimesberger
Production Assistant, Editorial: Deena Tucker
Designer: Ellen Ifrah

Library of Congress Cataloging-in-Publication Data

Verardo, Jennis Dennis.
   The Salinas Valley: an illustrated history/by Jennie Dennis
Verardo and Denzil Verardo. -- 1st ed.
   p.208 cm. 22x28
   "Produced in cooperation with the Salinas Chamber of Commerce."
   "Partners in progress, by John Waters": p. 136
   Bibliography: p. 203
   Includes index.
   ISBN 0-89781-309-X
   1. Salinas River Valley (Calif.)--History. 2. Salinas River Valley (Calif.)--
Description and travel--Views. 3. Salinas River Valley--Industries. 4. Salinas (Calif.)-
-History. 5. Salinas (Calif.)--Description--Views. 6. Salinas (Calif.)--Industries.
I. Verardo, Denzil. II. Salinas Chamber of Commerce. III. Title.
F868.S133V47 1989
979.4'76--dc19 89-30174 CIP

Windsor Publications, Inc.
Elliot Martin, Chairman of the Board
James L. Fish III, Chief Operating Officer
Michele Sylvestro, Vice President /Sales-Marketing

*Right: Main Street, Salinas, in the 1920s had
a modern look and sported this welcome sign.
Courtesy, Monterey County Historical Society*

*Frontispiece: This Salinas meadow basks un-
der a clear sky. Photo by Mark E. Gibson*

Contents

To our parents—
Claude and Beatrice Dennis
and
Richard and Florence Verardo

———

They each journeyed thousands of miles
and put in years of hard work to make their homes
and raise their families in this splendid Valley.
We are very grateful.

Digger pines in Pinnacles National Monument refresh the onlooker with their ever-green beauty. Photo by Lee Foster

Preface

The Salinas Valley is one of the most productive agricultural regions on earth. Its history is an exciting chronicle of the people and events that enabled the area to reach its agricultural potential. But it is also more than that, for much of the history of the Salinas Valley reflects the history of California and the West. California was, and is, unique. It offered the promise of dreams fulfilled, and although the promise was sometimes broken, the lure of the Golden State remained. The California "experience" would be different—poorer—without the Salinas Valley, for it was a significant part of the lure; part of the dream. It is with these facts in mind that we wrote this work, concentrating on the flow of California history as it affected the Valley, while focusing on the area's unique contributions to the broader historical record. And the contributions are many. From this perspective it is evident that the history of the Salinas Valley affords us an exciting window through which to view the growth and development of the people who made this region a land of green gold.

We have not written a definitive work on the Salinas Valley—there are still many facets to be explored—but we have written one that we hope is a readable, enjoyable, and accurate illustrated history, appealing to casual readers and serious historians alike. We have attempted to reach a level of enthusiasm in these pages reflective of the area's dynamic past.

As with any work of this magnitude, there are those without whom our task would have been more arduous, if not impossible. John Gross and Mary Gamble of the Salinas Steinbeck Library; Dallas Shaffer, Ruth Fornsberg, and Myra Kong at the Monterey County Library; and June Todd, Marlys Mayer, and Julie MacPherson with the Monterey County Historical Society offered us valuable assistance and every courtesy to make our research productive. Those three institutions are invaluable repositories of the historical records of the Salinas Valley.

Gaylord Nelson was not only a wealth of local information, but is appreciated for his constant optimism with respect to our work.

Alexander Lowry's photographic images and perspectives captured the spirit of the Salinas Valley. A true artist, we thank him for his continual catering to our requests.

Father Scott McCarthy of Our Lady of Refuge Catholic Church in Castroville allowed us to photograph the magnificent historic Trousset painting, which is the property of his parish and is reproduced as the cover jacket of this work.

There are many others whose assistance was appreciated including: Pat Hathaway, Robert Reese, Richard McKillop, and Kathy Wallace; the University of California, Santa Cruz, Special Collections; Sue Watson of the San Antonio Valley Historical Society and Lawrence Dinnean, Curator of Pictorial Collections at the Bancroft Library; Jerome and Peter Kasavan of Kasavan Associates; Lyle McKinsey and Sam McKinsey; Albert Pieri of the California Artichoke and Vegetable Growers Corporation; Andrew Ausonio of Ausonio Construction; and our patient editor, Kevin Taylor.

A special word of appreciation is due to Jean McCollister and the Salinas Chamber of Commerce, without whose sponsorship this work might not have been possible.

And, we thank our valued research assistant and son, Mark Verardo, for his efforts, assistance, patience, and support in accomplishing the research and preparation of this work.

—Jennie & Denzil Verardo
Castroville, California, 1988

During World War I the American Red Cross planned parades down Main Street in Salinas to stimulate the purchase of Liberty Bonds to aid the war effort. Salinas schoolchildren patriotically marched in the 1917 parade. Courtesy, Monterey County Library

8

CHAPTER ONE

"No Green Thing on the Plain"

The Salinas Valley for a hundred or more miles from the San Antonio hills, is a great plain ten to thirty miles wide. Great stretches are almost perfectly level, or have a very slight slope from the mountains to the river which winds through it. The ground was dry and parched and the very scanty grass was entirely dry. One saw no signs of vegetation at the first glance— that is, no green thing on the plain.

—William H. Brewer

Mission San Antonio, shown here in disrepair in 1914, was the first of three missions established in the Salinas Valley. Founded in 1771 by Father Junipero Serra, San Antonio became famous for the quality of the flour produced there. The main structure of Mission San Antonio was restored in the twentieth century. Today, San Antonio remains a part of the Catholic Church, and is one of the finest examples of a California mission in existence. Courtesy, Monterey County Library

Less than a century after William H. Brewer penned this description of the Salinas Valley in the 1860s, the "plain" was yielding one-tenth of the agricultural production of the United States. But long before its rich fertile soil felt the plow, or the water of its rivers was diverted for irrigation, or its resources were called upon to support towns and cities, forces were acting to change and shape the Salinas Valley.

Geologically speaking, the Salinas is a fairly young river valley. During the middle to late Pleis-

The Salinas River runs the length of Monterey County and is bounded by the Gabilan and Coast mountain ranges as illustrated in this 1881 map. One of North America's few south to north flowing rivers, it has the distinction of being the longest underground river in America. The valley formed by its flow is the largest intermontane valley on the California coast and was one of the first settled. Photo by Wallace Elliott

tocene period, uplifting and tilting of the northern end of the Gabilan Mountains changed a short, inconsequential stream into the Salinas River. Added geologic episodes and forces formed the present valley with its sedimentary, igneous, and metamorphic formations. The Salinas Valley is defined by the Santa Lucia and Sierra de Salinas mountain ranges on the west and southwest, and by the Gabilan Range, the Cholame Hills, and part of the Diablo Range on the east and northeast. The northwest-trending valley is, for the most part, in Monterey County, although the headwaters of the Salinas River lie well within San Luis Obispo County to the south.

The most significant feature of the Salinas Valley is the river from which it gets its name. The watershed of this 155-mile-long river consists of 4,000 square miles, creating the largest intermontane valley of the Coast Range. The Salinas

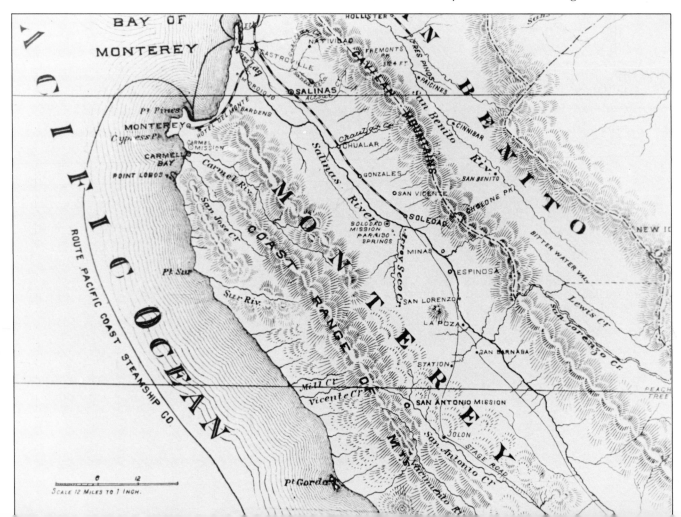

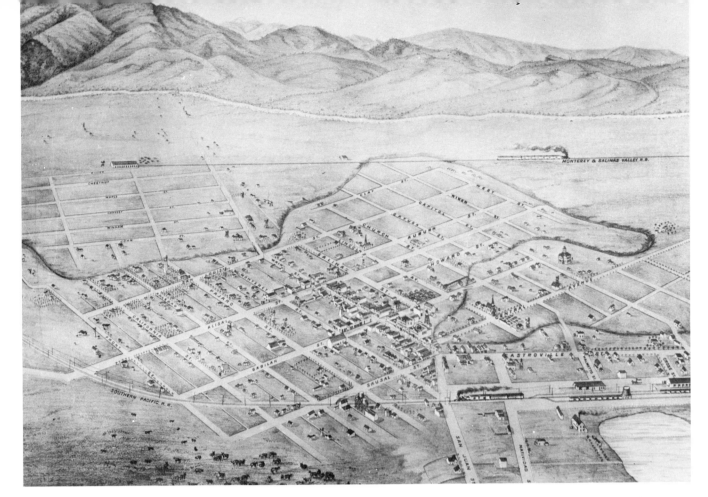

is fed by major tributaries consisting of the Naci-miento and San Antonio rivers in the southern portion of the Valley, the San Lorenzo River, which rises in the Gabilans and flows near King City, and the Arroyo Seco River farther north near Soledad.

The Salinas, which is considered the longest underground river in America because a substantial portion of its flow occurs below the surface, is a broad but fairly shallow river. In the twentieth century the river has entered Monterey Bay south of Moss Landing. However, in earlier times, accounts variously describe the mouth of the Salinas as sharing an outlet with the Pajaro and Elkhorn Slough; as being four kilometers north of Moss Landing; and occasionally, during severe flooding, as following its present course. The most widely accepted explanation for the permanent shift of the river mouth seems to be that during the winter storms of 1909-1910, the Salinas flowed due west into the bay, eliminating the sharp turn north near Mulligan Hill. Subsequently, the channel was diked by local farmers seeking to utilize the old riverbed. Another explanation that was popular for some time cited the 1906 earthquake as the cause for the change. How-

Above: The Costanoans, Salinans, and Esselens were native inhabitants of the Salinas Valley. By the time the first Europeans arrived, they had occupied various portions of the area. Gathering edible plants, hunting, and fishing supplied these Indian groups with their daily needs. Mortars, such as the bedrock mortar in this photograph, were used to grind acorns, a staple of the native diet, into meal. Photo by Lewis Slevin. Courtesy, Monterey County Library

Top: Salinas is not only the largest city in Monterey County, but also serves as the county seat. This nineteenth century photo highlights the city, as well as a cross section of the area's prominent geographical features. Courtesy, Pat Hathaway Photographs

ever, most current experts point out that because the "new" river mouth must be artificially maintained by dredging and diking, a unique situation has been perpetuated, and a major natural alteration has not occurred.

In the bay west of the present mouth of Elkhorn Slough lies another distinct geographical feature. The Monterey Submarine Canyon is the largest underwater canyon in western North America. This canyon is so immense that the Grand Canyon would fit in it. It is thought that during prehistoric times, the Elkhorn Slough area acted as a drainage outlet for the Santa Clara Valley as well as for the Central Valley. This large-scale drainage may have been a dominant force in the creation of the submarine canyon.

The canyon is a contributing factor in the weather conditions of much of the northern Salinas Valley. Cold water upwelling from the can-

Little evidence exists of the Salinas Valley's original Indian inhabitants. However, several artifacts, such as this mortar embedded in the exterior wall of the John Steinbeck Library in Salinas, provide clues to the native culture. Photo by Denzil Verardo. Courtesy, Denzil and Jennie Verardo

yon helps create the cool, damp fogs that are prevalent in the summer from Moss Landing up to Salinas. The canyon's influence ends there, however, and the same winds that carried the fog onshore then blow south, becoming the hot, dry winds that characterize summer conditions south of Chualar. Little or no rain falls during the summer. Totals from the rest of the year range from 21 inches near the coast to 9 inches at Soledad. Mild temperatures, low rainfall, and a long, frost-free growing season typify weather conditions in the Salinas Valley.

As significant as the river and the submarine canyon are, water was not the only physical force to affect the Valley. The San Andreas Fault, which is one of the most active and destructive in California, crosses the eastern part of the Salinas Valley, separating the Diablo Range from Gabilan Range and Cholame Hills. The earthquake activity level along this section of the fault is significant enough that in recent geologic time, displacement can be measured in miles, and the cumulative displacement may be hundreds of miles.

In addition to movement along the San Andreas and several other active faults, the Valley

has also been subjected to folding, which has produced the geologic structures responsible for local accumulation of oil, especially near San Ardo.

The area east of Soledad known as the Pinnacles was, at one time, a vigorous volcanic field. Evidence of the violent creation of that portion of the Gabilan Range is still apparent today. Spires, pinnacles, and crags are obvious remnants of the prehistoric lava flow, forming a landscape so unique that the Pinnacles was made a national monument in 1908.

The first humans to dwell in this vast and beautiful valley were divided into three distinct groups. The Costanoans occupied the area along the coast and inland upvalley to a point south of Soledad. This represented a relatively small portion of the Costanoans' range, which extended from San Francisco Bay to south of Monterey Bay. Arriving more than 2,000 years ago, the Costanoans found a land rich in plant and animal resources, and nearby, an equally rich marine environment in the bay and sloughs. The ability to supply their needs through hunting, fishing, and gathering meant they lacked the need for developing more advanced skills such as agriculture or animal domestication.

South of the Costanoans, in the Salinas Valley and along the adjacent coastline, was the territory of the Salinan group. Described by the early Spanish explorer Pedro Fages as "gentle and affable," he noted that they "willingly divide with the Spanish the little they have," and also credited them with being, "well built, and the women are good looking . . ." Given the ready availability of food in the Valley and along the coast, the Salinans appear to have had little reason to travel except for occasional trips between the coast and valley and to Tulare Lake for fishing. Acorns were a staple of their diet. Like the Costanoans, the Salinans were faced with little need to develop intensive skills other than gathering, hunting, and fishing. Basketry seems to have been their only manufacturing activity.

Right: Gabriel, an Indian born in 1771, died in 1890 at the age of 119. Having lived in the Salinas Valley near Natividad in the latter half of the nineteenth century, he witnessed Spanish, Mexican, and American period changes. Though it is unknown whether Gabriel was a local or came from the Central Valley, he represented the decline of the native population in the Salinas Valley. Courtesy, Monterey County Library

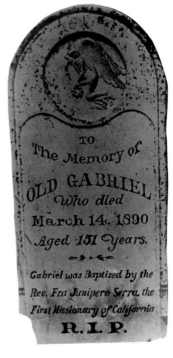

Left: Upon his death in 1890, Gabriel was buried in the cemetery at Mission San Carlos in Carmel. Courtesy, Monterey County Library

This adobe, located on Boronda Road in Salinas, is the headquarters of the Monterey County Historical Society. Built by Don Jose Eusebio Boronda, who was the son of a member of the Portola expedition, the Boronda adobe is one of the Valley's few Mexican-era structures open to the public. Courtesy, Monterey County Historical Society

The third group of native inhabitants of the Salinas Valley was the Esselen. Little is known about this group, the least populous of the three. They did control the upper reaches of the Arroyo Seco and Carmel rivers and probably numbered 500 to 750.

Aside from the occasional use of fire as a land and game management technique, the native inhabitants of the Salinas Valley did little to change the land. They lived a harmonious coexist-ence with the natural environment, taking only what was needed for subsistence and leaving little, other than small refuse mounds or middens, to mark their tenure there. For more than a thousand years these peoples hunted antelope near Soledad, fished the Salinas and other rivers for trout and steelhead, and collected shellfish near Moss Landing. Territories were not marked on a map and life here seems to have been a relatively good and uncomplicated journey.

The same bountiful serenity that provided for the Costanoans, Salinans, and Esselens eventually attracted Europeans, and inexorably changed the way life would be lived in this Valley.

California became part of the Spanish empire. In relation to Spain's vast holdings in the New World, the Salinas Valley was considered part of the northern frontier: an unexplored outpost in the marginal colony of California. In 1493 the pope issued a decree dividing the world's uncharted lands between two powerful Catholic exploring nations, Spain and Portugal. Spain received uncompetitive control of all but a relatively small portion of the Western Hemisphere.

At first, pressure for colonization was lacking. Some exploration did occur, but these efforts, while individually remarkable, were few and far between. Juan Rodriguez Cabrillo's venture up the California coast in 1542, Sebastian Cermeño's exploration down the coast from San Francisco in 1595, and Sebastian Vizcaino's voyage in 1602 were some of the notable early endeavors. By the latter half of the eighteenth century, however, Spain no longer enjoyed monopolistic control of this part of the globe. The British were pirating Spanish shipping, and foreign trappers were venturing overland into California itself. Perhaps most alarming to Spain was the Russian advance that eventually culminated with the establishment of Fort Ross in 1812.

The Spanish Crown ordered authorities in New Spain to assess the Russian danger. In 1768 Jose Galvez, the king's Visitor-General in Mexico, ordered an expedition, led by Don Gaspar de Portola, governor of Baja (Lower) California, north to find Monterey Bay, which had been favorably described by Vizcaino's earlier exploration. Portola was accompanied by the president of the Baja missions, Father Junipero Serra. In 1769 Portola and Serra arrived in Alta (Upper) California and founded Mission San Diego de Alcala, but before long their situation grew desperate. Many of the members of Portola's expedition had died en route, and most of the survivors were ill. They decided, however, to continue their quest. Serra remained in San Diego to care for the ill, while Portola moved north accompanied by Captain Fernando Rivera y Moncada, Lieutenant Pedro Fages, Father Juan Crespi, and Miguel Costanso, the party's cartographer.

The Portola party left San Diego on July 14, 1769, and followed a route northward along the

Famed Spanish explorer Juan Bautista de Anza traveled the length of the Salinas Valley in 1776, as part of his trek from Mexico to San Francisco, California. This map shows the route of the Anza expedition through the Salinas Valley, as well as that portion of the National Park Service's proposed Anza National Historical Trail route. Courtesy, National Park Service

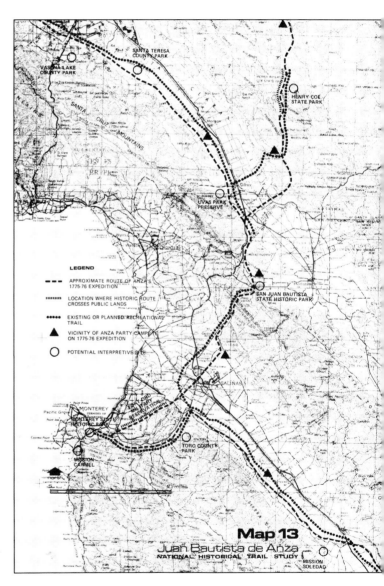

Mission Nuestra Senora de la Soledad was founded on October 9, 1791, by Father Lasuen, who replaced Father Junipero Serra, upon Serra's death, as head of California's missions. Soledad was poorly constructed and, for a time, poorly administered, which contributed to its demise. Much of Mission Soledad remains in ruins. Photo by Denzil Verardo. Courtesy, Denzil and Jennie Verardo

coast until they found their way blocked by the Santa Lucia mountain range. Turning inland, they began to cross this barrier. After several days of slow, arduous travel, Father Crespi commented that the endless mountains presented "a sad spectacle for poor travellers worn out by the fatigues of so long a journey."

On September 24, Portola's band finally arrived at the San Antonio River near Jolon. Two days later they reached the Salinas River. Originally the party called the river the "Rio Del Carmelo," but later christened it the "Rio de San Elizario." Following the river, the party journeyed down the Salinas Valley and after six days finally camped near its mouth. Ascending Mulligan Hill near Castroville to view the area, Portola's men did not recognize the bay Vizcaino had exaggeratedly glorified.

The chroniclers of the expedition noted that the Salinas River was too deep to ford at its mouth, and also noted an estuary that the river flowed into before entering the Pacific Ocean.

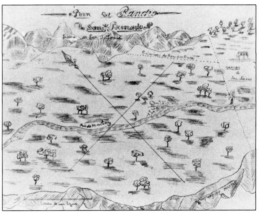

The band then continued north, discovering San Francisco Bay, and returned by the same route, arriving in San Diego in January 1770.

The members of the Portola expedition had not achieved their immediate objective, but had become the first Europeans to explore the Salinas Valley.

Undaunted by his original failure, Portola again marched north and rendezvoused with the Spanish vessel *San Antonio* in Monterey, having this time "found" the bay. On June 3, 1770, a presidio and mission were established and Pedro Fages was put in command of the government of Alta California by Portola.

In November 1770 Fages led an expedition to the Salinas River. Fages left a revealing description of the area. He stated that they saw "many bear's trails," as well as "many flocks of geese," and that the area near the river mouth was "thickly grown with alders, live-oaks, and other trees."

By 1773 California had two presidios and five missions, including Mission San Antonio in the Salinas Valley, staffed by a small force of soldiers and friars. Spanish authorities now felt it imperative that an efficient land route be opened to Alta California to provision the new settlements. The individual commissioned to carry out

Above: With Mexican independence from Spain in 1822, numerous land grants were given by the new government to loyal citizens upon petition. Since no offical surveyors existed in Mexican California, the petitioner would describe the land sought with as much detail as possible. Several individuals included sketches with their request; the sketch shown here accompanied the petition for Rancho San Bernardo, near present-day San Ardo. The Rio de Monterey is the Salinas River. Courtesy, Denzil and Jennie Verardo

Top: Mission San Miguel was founded by Father Lasuen on July 25, 1797. It was the third and final mission established in the Salinas Valley. During the Mexican War in 1846, John Charles Fremont, famous in California for his adventures, stopped at Mission San Miguel to provision his California Battalion en route to Southern California. Sketch by Henry Miller. Courtesy, The Bancroft Library

this task was Captain Juan Bautista de Anza.

Leaving Mexico in 1774 with a group of colonists for Alta California, Anza entered the Salinas Valley in 1776. On March 6 he stopped at Mission San Antonio. From San Antonio, Anza followed a route along the Salinas River, passing the sites of present-day King City, Greenfield, Soledad, and Spreckels. He continued his journey through Monterey to San Francisco Bay before returning to Mexico.

The Salinas Valley was one of the first valleys in California to be settled by the Spaniards. Their occupation of California had been gradual but effective. Through exploration and missionization, Spain gained control of more than half of the territory's coastal belt.

Three of California's 21 missions were in the Salinas Valley. Mission San Antonio de

Adobe construction served proprietors in Mexican California well. Bricks made from dirt, straw, and water were stacked to form walls, and roofs were covered with tiles or wood. Adobes dotted the Salinas Valley landscape during the Mexican and early American periods. Photo by Lewis Slevin. Courtesy, Monterey County Library

Padua was California's third mission, following the founding of San Diego and Carmel. In July 1771 Father Junipero Serra led a small band from Mission Carmel up the Salinas Valley to a site on the San Antonio River, which, the Portola expedition had noted, would be a good spot for a mission.

The location was chosen because it possessed water for irrigation (a precious commodity in the upland areas of the Valley during summer), a suitable building site, and sufficient grazing land. When the Anza expedition stopped at Mission San Antonio on its trek north, they were impressed by it, confirming the belief that the site could be successful.

Junipero Serra's contemporary chronicler, Father Palou, compiled the first report on California's missions. In 1773 he documented that San Antonio, a year and a half after its founding, had a church, dwellings, and cultivated fields, and that the fathers had baptized 158 people. Palou revealed considerable detail on the lifestyles of both the missionary fathers and the Indians associated with Mission San Antonio. Palou wrote that, "the gentiles subsist on wild seeds which

they obtain in the extensive cañada, such as acorns . . . rabbit flesh, also flesh of squirrels, which are not of worse quality or taste."

The second mission founded in the Salinas Valley was Nuestra Señora de la Soledad on October 9, 1791, by Fray Fermin Francisco de Lasuen. Lasuen had taken control of California's missions upon the death of Father Serra.

Unlike San Antonio, Soledad seemed to suffer misfortune from the start. The area was cold and damp in winter, and had desiccating summer winds. The soil was not conducive to making sturdy adobe bricks; those that were made continually deteriorated. The native population was not large and therefore labor was in short supply.

Two of the padres assigned to Soledad were also anomalies among the normally devout Franciscans. Fathers Mariano Rubi and Bartolome Gili were noted for their outrageous behavior. Both had attended the Franciscan College of San Fernando in Mexico City, where it was documented that they created great disturbances which included scaling the walls in the evening to spend the night in town. They complained constantly of their duty at Soledad and wanted to be removed. Father Lasuen finally allowed both to leave.

Rubi and Gili were replaced by Father Sarria, who was as devout and dedicated as Rubi and Gili were impious. But even his loyal industry could not make Soledad a successful mission.

The third and final mission founded in the Salinas Valley was Mission San Miguel. Father Lasuen dedicated it on July 25, 1797.

With the establishment of the missions, agricultural production, though limited, was begun in the Salinas Valley. Corn, wheat, beans, and barley were some of the crops planted and harvested but, "every kind of garden plant thrives astonishingly," said the Frenchman La Perouse on his visit to the area.

Mission San Antonio was especially famous for its wheat and flour. In 1815, when Governor Pablo Sola visited Monterey, it was the cele-

In 1836 Juan Bautista Alvarado led a successful revolt against the current governor and filled that post himself until 1842. Governor Alvarado built this adobe in the Salinas Valley. Courtesy, Denzil and Jennie Verardo

brated flour from Mission San Antonio that was used to make the cakes for the feast honoring him.

Besides agricultural activities, livestock production was developing in the Salinas Valley. Mission San Antonio was noted for its excellent horses. Cattle and other livestock supplemented the provisions provided by supply ships that arrived in Monterey from San Blas, Mexico.

Preventing the flight of Indians from the missions was a constant problem. In 1815 a "grand expedition," led by the Spaniard Juan Ortega, left Mission San Miguel to round up and return Indians who had escaped from the missions. After several weeks the party returned, having captured a total of nine prisoners!

Ironically, while the missions, along with the presidios and pueblos, were stabilizing the frontier in California, Spain was already destined to lose its empire. The Spanish fleet in Europe had come under the control of France. Spain rebelled against France in 1808; the two were locked in a bitter struggle for five years, until the French armies were driven from Spain. Throughout the Napoleonic period, Spain could hardly af-

ford to give much attention to its colonies.

In 1818 the privateer Hippolyte de Bouchard, flying the flag of Buenos Aires (Argentina), attacked Monterey. Bouchard claimed to be operating for the cause of the revolution against Spain. Anticipating Bouchard's landing, families were sent to Mission Soledad and Governor Sola pulled his Spanish force back to the site of present-day Salinas. After ransacking Monterey and the presidio there, Bouchard left without engaging Sola's reinforced contingent.

The disenchantment with Spain felt by its distant colonists resulted in a revolt by Mexico against Spanish rule. This culminated with independence for Mexico in 1822.

Following the revolution, the Mexican government made generous land grants to loyal citizens in Alta California. These ranchos served to further settle the Salinas Valley. Prior to Mexican independence, Spain had issued concessions to settlers, but these, while often called land grants, were actually little more than grazing permits; title remained vested with the Spanish Crown. Most of these were located in the lower Salinas Valley. However, Mexican grants virtually lined the Salinas Valley with ranchos, many of which comprised several thousand acres.

In the 1830s Mexico secularized the missions of California, an action which in essence took most of the holdings from the Church and placed them in civil hands. Not only was Church control diminished in the Salinas Valley, but more land was now available for granting to the growing civilian population.

Cattle raising, begun by the Spanish to supplement supplies, flourished in the Valley during Mexican rule. Californians could not consume all the meat produced, so trade in hides and tallow became a major economic activity for the Valley's missions and ranchos alike. These commodities were traded to merchants for many essential, as well as luxury, items.

Two of the first traders to arrive in the area were William Edward Petty Hartnell and Hugh McCulloch, representing the English commercial firm of John Begg and Company. Hartnell and McCulloch negotiated a monopoly for the hide and tallow trade, taking all the hides and tallow the Salinas Valley, as well as other parts of California, could produce. Soon, however, other merchants appeared on the scene and trade became increasingly competitive.

In 1823-1824 a drought occurred in the area which caused the death of thousands of cattle as grass shriveled. Several thousand horses were slaughtered at Mission Soledad in an attempt to preserve valuable pasture for the cattle. Even with loss from drought, it is estimated that between 1800 and 1848 over 5,000,000 hides were traded in California!

William E.P. Hartnell's career created a much greater historic contribution than the hide and tallow trade. Hartnell was born in England in 1798 and arrived in South America in 1819, where he resided for a few years. A brilliant scholar, Hartnell had mastered Spanish in the 10 weeks it took to sail across the Atlantic.

Hartnell was baptized a Catholic at Mission San Carlos (Carmel) in 1824, and married Maria Teresa de la Guerra in 1825. In 1827, due in no small part to his fluency in Spanish, Hartnell was appointed British Vice Consul in Monterey. Several years later he became the sole representative of the Russian-American Fur Company in Mexican territory.

Always eager to read, learn, and teach, Hartnell tutored Juan Bautista Alvarado, who was destined to become governor of Mexican California, as well as General Mariano Vallejo, one of California's most noted and respected residents.

Facing page: Isaac Graham, a trapper and early California settler, assisted Juan Alvarado with his successful revolt against Governor Nicolas Gutierrez. Graham operated a distillery at Natividad, northeast of Salinas, and had a reputation as being incorrigible. Fearing an overthrow himself, Alvarado eventually had Graham and his followers imprisoned and sent to Mexico. Courtesy, Denzil and Jennie Verardo

California's first public school of higher education was established by William Hartnell in 1834. Although the adobe school was officially named El Colegio de San Jose, it was often called Hartnell's school. Hartnell, originally from England, had married and settled in the Salinas Valley. His linguistic abilities in Spanish as well as English earned him not only acclaim as an educator in Mexican California, but also as an interpreter. Hartnell's adobe is shown here prior to its destruction in 1960. Courtesy, Monterey County Historical Society

In 1830 Hartnell swore allegiance to Mexico and became a citizen of California in order to obtain a rancho and relinquish the precarious economic life of a trader. He was granted the Alisal Rancho, east of Salinas, and there, in 1834, established the first public college in California.

William Hartnell also served as tax collector; as "Visitador de Misiones," a special assignment by Governor Alvarado to investigate the state of the missions; as chief of customs; and as an interpreter for foreigners calling on the government of Mexican California. This Salinas Valley resident also acted as an interpreter during the questioning of American Commodore Thomas ap Catesby Jones, who mistakingly "captured" Monterey in 1842 and lowered the Mexican flag.

Hartnell later was chosen to translate for California's Constitutional Convention; to become a justice of the peace; to translate a portion of the first issue of California's first English-language newspaper, the *Californian*, into Spanish for bilingual reading; and to serve on California's first impaneled jury. William Hartnell was a force not only in the history of the Salinas Valley, but in the history of California as well.

The romantic era of the Mexican rancho was relatively short-lived in the Salinas Valley. The process of secularization, which had freed land for settlement and diminished the power of the Church, also weakened Mexico's hold on its northern province.

American interest in California was growing. Settlers pushed across the United States toward California; merchants and mountain men had already arrived. Mountain men James Ohio Pattie, Ewing Young, and Jedediah Smith had traversed the Salinas Valley in their explorations, and foreigners, like Hartnell, had become permanent settlers.

The United States government had become increasingly aware of California during the 1840s, and came to believe that inadequate Mexican control of Alta California might encourage British seizure of the area. The U.S. did not want England,

Originally built in the 1820s, near what would become the Spreckels refinery, the Rancho Buena Vista adobe, seen here circa 1920, no longer exists. This once proud, two-story dwelling represents the close of the Mexican period. With the coming of American soldiers and settlers, adobe was soon replaced by other building materials. Photo by Lewis Slevin. Courtesy, Monterey County Library

or any other European power, to extend their influence in North America.

John C. Fremont was sent west on several "scientific" survey expeditions by the U.S. government. In 1846 he was in the Sacramento Valley, where he wanted to remain for the winter. Fremont traveled to Monterey to obtain the necessary permit, but instead of heading back to the Central Valley he camped on Hartnell's Alisal Rancho. Fremont was ordered out of the territory, but instead moved to the top of Hawk's Peak (today Fremont Peak) and raised a U.S. flag.

The Mexican commander, General Manuel Castro, gathered a force of several hundred men to march on Fremont. Fremont retreated toward Sacramento, where he avoided conflict, as he had been instructed by the U.S. government.

However, war soon broke out between the United States and Mexico. Fremont enlisted volunteers from among the American settlers in California and formed the California Battalion of Mounted Riflemen.

Upon arrival in Monterey, which was now in U.S. hands, Fremont was commissioned a lieutenant colonel and given orders to secure men and horses for the war in Southern California. While in Monterey, a band of Fremont's men was driving horses from San Juan Bautista to Monterey, and, at Rancho La Natividad, northeast of present-day Salinas, was attacked by a California force lead by Manuel Castro.

This "Battle of Natividad" was the only mil-

Below and facing page: The adobes of the Salinas Valley took on many different functions. These were used as storage sheds, simple residences, and ranch houses. Few of the once-dominant structures remain today, victims of both neglect and the elements.
Courtesy, Monterey County Library

itary engagement fought in Northern California during the Mexican War. Thomas O. Larkin, the American consul in Monterey who had been captured the day before and brought to Castro's camp on the Salinas River, was a spectator to the battle. After the engagement, Larkin was taken south toward Los Angeles by Castro's forces.

Fremont also moved south through the Salinas Valley with his battalion of mounted riflemen. The entire expedition was chronicled by Edwin Bryant, a first lieutenant with Fremont. The trek was arduous as rain and cold, deep mud, and swollen Salinas River tributaries hampered their advance. Bryant's keen observations have left an excellent description of the Salinas Valley in 1846. He described the area as not being adapted for any agricultural purpose except grazing, but said that California beef was, "fat, juicy, and tender, and surpasses in flavor any which I have tasted elsewhere." The Salinas Valley, "as it approaches the ocean, is broad and fertile, and there are many fine ranchos upon it. But higher up, the stream becomes dry in the summer, and the soil of the valley is arid and sandy."

Fremont quartered his men on a rancho near Soledad (now Los Coches Rancho State Historic Monument), where he left a large unpaid bill. By the time they reached Mission San Miguel, Fremont's battalion was out of beef and forced to feast on mutton from the mission.

Edwin Bryant put perhaps the best contemporary wartime perspective on the battalion when he wrote that "the men composing the California Battalion . . . are roughly clad, and weather beaten in their exterior appearance; but I feel it but justice here to state my belief, that no military party ever passed through an enemy's country and observed the same strict regard for the rights of its population . . . the deportment of the battalion might be cited as a model for imitation."

By the time Fremont left the Salinas Valley, he had lost 80 horses due to insufficient grass, and the entire battalion had to advance on foot.

Persevering, Fremont's forces did reach their southern destination.

On January 13, 1847, Andres Pico capitulated to Fremont at Cahuenga, ending hostilities. In February 1848 the Treaty of Guadalupe Hidalgo formally ended the Mexican War.

California was now a territory of the United States.

CHAPTER TWO

Beyond the County Seat

The air was filled with dry dust and sand, so that we could not see the hills at the side, the fine sand stinging our faces like shot, the air as dry as if it had come from a furnace . . . Our lips cracked and bled, our eyes were bloodshot, our skins smarting. If it is thus in May, what must it be here in . . . August!

—*from* Brewer's Journal

One of the proud names associated with the Mexican heritage of the Salinas Valley was Boronda. Eusebio Boronda had been granted 2,230 acres by Governor Alvarado in 1840. In 1854 Boronda's title to the land was confirmed by the Land Commission, and later by the U.S. District Court. In this 1915 photograph, Eusebio's son, Francisco Boronda, stands with his two granddaughters, Sophie and Leone. Courtesy, Monterey County Historical Society

The Salinas Valley in the 1850s was sparsely populated. In 1849 a constitutional convention was convened in Monterey, with William Hartnell acting in the key role of translator between English- and Spanish-speaking delegates. The California constitution was completed in 1849, and California was admitted to the Union in 1850. Monterey County became one of California's original 27 counties. Outside of the city of Monterey, which at that time was the county seat, there were less than 800 people in the entire county. Those who did reside in the Salinas Valley lived on the ranchos that had been granted under Mexican rule. The Treaty of Guadalupe Hidalgo guaranteed the property rights of the owners of these ranchos, but the new American settlers coming to Gold Rush California demanded land for settle-

ment. In 1851 Congress passed an act creating a three-man land commission to examine all titles issued by Mexico in order to open the public domain for settlement while preserving valid land grants.

Monterey County did have its own "Mother Lode," which for a time promised wealth to those who sought it, but the county's mines never created the wealth secured in the Sierra Nevada mines. In the 1850s both placer and hard-rock mining took place in the Santa Lucia mountains between Mission San Antonio and the coast, but it was not until 1869 that a significant yield was documented. In that year, one account lists $100,000 worth of gold removed from the area.

In 1875 the Los Burros Mining District was formed and 63 claims were registered. By the 1880s, 500 claims had been recorded. Removing the ore from the area was no easy task since the barrier formed by the Santa Lucias was the same rugged terrain that had hindered the Portola expedition 100 years earlier.

To transport ore out of the area, the ore had to be broken up and packed out to a point

Below, left: Even after the turn of the century, remnants of Jolon's past were evident, as Jolon pioneer settlers Charles Blanchard and Ed Dutton attested when they posed with this nineteenth-century cart. As grain markets increased, the Jolon area became an important agricultural area, though it never developed as an urban community. Courtesy, Monterey County Library

where it could be loaded onto wagons bound for King City. From there it would be transferred to a train and shipped to San Francisco for processing.

On the opposite side of the Valley, coal mining also flourished briefly with the establishment of the Monterey Coal Mining Company in 1874. The difficulties in removing coal in the Gabilan Range were similar to those encountered in removing gold from the Los Burros mines, and the enterprise was equally short-lived. It was in agriculture that the Salinas Valley's future fortunes would be found.

Due to the increased demand for beef caused by the Gold Rush, the Salinas Valley's rancheros prospered. During the previous era the hide and tallow trade had relied on large herds of cattle, but little could be done with the beef itself. Now meat was in great demand. Great cattle drives were made through the area en route to San Francisco and the goldfields. In 1856 over 36,000 head of cattle passed the Natividad Post Office alone!

Soon, however, the market created by the Gold Rush was oversupplied and the fortunes of the ranchos began to decline. Beef prices became so ruinous that cattle once again were slaughtered only for their hides and tallow. The early 1860s brought further hardship to the industry. In the winter of 1861-1862 enormous flooding occurred, killing stock and destroying valuable pasturage. This flooding was followed, in 1862-1863 and 1863-1864, by two consecutive, disastrous droughts. Over 50,000 head of cattle were eliminated due to the lack of viable pasture for the animals.

Left: In 1849 Antonio Ramirez built an adobe inn in the San Antonio Valley for travelers passing through the area. The site soon became a stage stop and, with the discovery of gold in the Santa Lucia Mountains, the small settlement of Jolon grew. Jolon was an important crossroad for the Los Burros Mining District traffic bound for King City. George Dutton acquired the inn property and opened the two-story Dutton Hotel, seen here. The remnants of the hotel are a designated National Historic Landmark. Courtesy, Monterey County Historical Society

Below: The Salinas Valley had long been subject to periodic flooding. The disastrous winter of 1861-1862, which destroyed valuable pasturage, contributed to a decline in the area's cattle industry. Flooding continued to be a serious threat to the economy well into the twentieth century, as this 1920 photo confirms. Courtesy, Monterey County Historical Society

Many ranchos were mortgaged in order to cope with this financial disaster. The breakup of these ranchos was hastened not only by serious economic problems, but also by the ever-increasing demand for land for homesteading and settlement. The 8,875-acre Rancho San Lucas was sold for $3,000 in 1861; Rancho Sauzal's 10,000 acres were purchased for $600; Rancho El Alisal was auctioned; and the 13,000-acre Rancho San Bernabe was sold for $500.

The blueprint for the Salinas Valley's settlement pattern was drawn during this important period. Rancho San Bernardo, encompassing both sides of the Salinas River in the San Ardo area, illustrates both the sequence of events and the cultural changes that occurred throughout the area.

Jose Mariano Soberanes was born in the late 1790s and served as a soldier from 1819 to 1821. In 1823, 1829, and 1830 he was the alcalde in Monterey, and in 1835 he was the administrator of Mission San Antonio. With secularization of the missions, San Antonio's vast holdings were opened for land grants by the Mexican government. In 1840, on behalf of two of his sons, Soberanes petitioned Governor Alvarado for a portion of the land and was granted title to 13,346 acres of San Antonio's holdings.

With American control of California, Soberanes' claim to Rancho San Bernardo, as his land grant was called, was upheld by both the Land Commission and the United States District Court. But the economic problems of the 1860s forced the sale of the rancho, and it ended up in the hands of M. Brandenstein and Company of San Francisco. Brandenstein had numerous head of cattle, and grew enough wheat and barley not only to supply his herd, but also to ship large quantities out of the area. The community of San Ardo was established in the 1880s by Brandenstein, and a depot and warehouse were constructed after the Southern Pacific Railroad extended its route through that area. Brandenstein eventually sold portions of this ranch to other settlers, resulting in the settlement patterns we are familiar with in the twentieth century.

Some of the new American entrepreneurs actually wound up with landholdings in the Salinas Valley larger than any of the earlier Mexican grants. Henry Miller and Charles Lux formed the Miller and Lux Company and eventually amassed some three million acres in the West! The Miller and Lux Company acquired their property in a variety of ways, but many land grants were purchased by the company from heirs who

could not afford to keep the property. Rancho San Lorenzo, east of King City, was the center of their Peach Tree Ranch, which contained over 45,000 acres.

Similarly, William Randolph Hearst acquired three ranchos, formerly part of Mission San Miguel's lands. His holdings would total some 240,000 acres in Monterey and San Luis Obispo counties. A large part of his ranch in the Salinas River watershed became, in 1940, the Hunter Liggett Military Reservation.

The lifestyle of the ranchero of Mexican California had ended abruptly.

Although Monterey County would continue to be one of the leading cattle producers in California, in the Salinas Valley grain began to replace cattle as the predominant agricultural commodity, and the number of sheep increased because sheep could better handle drought conditions. For the first time, the fencing of land to confine herds became widespread, facilitating an increase in farming.

During the 1840s wheat had become a more abundant crop throughout California. Most wheat had been harvested by Indians and threshed by horses, but as grain production increased, threshing machines replaced Indian workers. The milling of wheat went through a similar transition as Indian metates were re-

Above and top: Grain became increasingly important in the Salinas Valley in the late nineteenth century. Large wagons were pulled by horses, and threshing machines replaced the Indian labor that had been used initially in the production of wheat. Soon wheat became the major agricultural enterprise in the area. These early photos illustrate the "technology" used in grain production during the late nineteenth century. Courtesy, Monterey County Historical Society

Facing page: The economic problems of the 1860s forced many early Mexican settlers to sell their ranchos. Jose Mariano Soberanes was forced to sell Rancho San Bernardo to M. Brandenstein & Co. of San Francisco. Brandenstein established the community of San Ardo, shown here, upon that land in the 1800s. Courtesy, Monterey County Historical Society

Stages like this one, which appeared in the 1924 California Rodeo, plied the Salinas Valley in the latter half of the nineteenth century. They were a vital boon to communications as they provided a valuable link between the area's communities. Occasionally they also provided a "boon" to stagecoach robbers. The Coastline Stage was held up by two men outside of Soledad and the express box was taken. A $250 reward was offered for the robbers' arrest and conviction. Courtesy, Monterey County Library

placed by simple mills. William Heath Davis, in *Seventy-Five Years in California,* left a firsthand account of this period's technology when he wrote, "the ranchero made his flour by crushing the wheat by means of an apparatus composed of two circular stones a yard in diameter . . . a shaft being affixed to the upper stone and turned by mule power."

During this time, the Salinas Valley had virtu-

ally no transportation systems capable of carrying the farmers' wheat to distant markets. The California Stage Company began service through Natividad and Salinas as early as 1855. Between 1848 and 1854 William Richardson had maintained his adobe as a station for the San Juan and Soledad Stage at what is today Los Coches Rancho State Historic Monument. That roadhouse also served as a stop, between 1854 and 1868, for the Bixby Overland Stage, which ran between San Francisco and Los Angeles. In 1866 the Coast Line Stage Company also operated through the Salinas Valley en route to Los Angeles. But these routes, while a boon to communication, were of little commercial value to the farmer.

Finally, in 1866, terminal facilities were developed by Captain Charles Moss, at the landing that now bears his name. By 1881 Moss Landing

was capable of storing 15,000 tons of grain. From Moss Landing this grain could be shipped to major transportation facilities such as those at San Francisco. During this same period, the Civil War created an increased demand for grain, as Britain, cut off from the East, turned to the West Coast, to California, to supply her needs.

The Southern Pacific Railroad extended its line south from San Francisco, reaching Salinas in 1872 and Soledad in 1873. Southern Pacific's freight rates, however, were high and cut into agricultural profits. Two Monterey County entrepreneurs, David Jacks and Carlisle Abbott, decided to compete with Southern Pacific, building a narrow-gage railroad line between the port at Monterey and Salinas.

Their narrow-gage enterprise struggled, however. Poor weather reduced crops to the point where little was available for shipping. Abbott mortgaged his property and Jacks took out a loan to keep the railroad operating. Finally, the line was sold to Southern Pacific at bankruptcy proceedings, consolidating SP's monopoly in the Salinas Valley.

Flour mills were operating in the 1880s in both King City and Salinas, and, by 1890, gravity irrigation was begun on a commercial basis by the San Bernardo and Salinas Valley Canal and Irrigation Company.

As grain and flour production increased,

Top: Between 1840 and 1860, Salinas Valley farmers had severe difficulty getting their wheat to distant markets. Therefore, much of the area's grain had to be used locally, and oversupply resulted. Finally, in 1866, Captain Charles Moss, after whom Moss Landing is named, developed terminal facilities which were capable of storing 15,000 tons of grain. Photo by Lewis Slevin. Courtesy, Monterey County Library

Above: The horse and buggy provided early Valley settlers with their only available means of calling on their neighbors, getting supplies, and traveling as families between communities. The numbers of early roads and bridges, often impassable in winter, increased dramatically as more and more settlers arrived. Courtesy, Pat Hathaway Photographs

A scene such as this would have been common in Moss Landing in the late 1860s after Captain Charles Moss developed his shipping facilities. Moss Landing became a focal point for socializing as farmers chatted with one another while unloading their wares. Courtesy, Orange County Marine Institute

dairy herds began to build up. Cheese and butter production increased to the point where factory facilities became profitable, and alfalfa could be grown to improve the quality of milk. After the turn of the century, John Meyenberg, who invented the evaporated milk process, opened a plant in Gonzales because of the availability of dairy animals.

Unlike the cattle industry in the Salinas Valley, the sheep industry expanded after the droughts of the 1860s. When William Brewer surveyed the Salinas Valley in that decade he noted large flocks, including one which "contained not less than 6,000 sheep." By 1870 the county was the leading wool-producing area in California. However, as grain markets and profits increased, aided by improved transportation, the Valley's sheep ranches also began to be replaced by wheat fields.

Production of wheat in California peaked in 1884 and by 1889 began to decline as stronger midwestern wheats became more desirable and foreign production increased. But by this time agriculture in the Salinas Valley had begun to diversify,

Top: Dairy production became an important economic activity in the Salinas Valley toward the end of the nineteenth century. Gonzales, in particular, became known for its dairy herds as Italian-Swiss settlers arrived with improved stock. Due to the availability of dairy animals, cheese and butter processing plants were built in the area. The Alpine Evaporative Cream Company, shown here, was opened in Gonzales by John Meyenburg, who invented the evaporated milk process. Courtesy, Denzil and Jennie Verardo

Above: Sheep became profitable in the Salinas Valley during the second half of the nineteenth century because they could better withstand the droughts which devastated the area's cattle economy. By the 1870s Monterey County was the leading wool-producing area in California. Later, however, as grain markets and profits increased, sheep ranches were replaced by wheat fields, and agricultural products dominated the Salinas Valley. Courtesy, Monterey County Historical Society

hastened by the declining demand for wheat. Alfalfa, sugar beets, barley, beans, and potatoes were planted. Diversification in turn led to a greater demand for reliable water sources. In 1897 the Spreckels Sugar Company installed steam-powered pumping plants near Soledad and King City, and wells were drilled to tap underground sources. As the availability of irrigated land increased, agriculture became more intensive, paving the way for the planting of lettuce, and other row crops, in the next century.

Rancho Bolsa del Protrero y Moro Cojo, encompassing the Castroville area, which the Mexican government granted to Captain J.R. Cooper of Boston in 1828, exemplified the Valley's agricultural changes. Cattle raising began as the principal economic activity but was replaced in the 1860s by wheat and barley. In 1888 sugar beets were grown on the property and in the 1920s artichokes were planted, an event that ultimately led

to Castroville becoming the "Artichoke Capital of the World," a distinction it retains today.

As the Salinas Valley's agricultural possibilities developed, its rural communities grew with the corresponding influx of new settlers.

Prior to the name Moss Landing, the coastal town at the mouth of the Valley was called the City of St. Paul. St. Paul was actually a 300-acre subdivision, one of the Valley's first, laid out by Paul Lezere. Lezere also constructed a ferry landing and roads. On October 25, 1877, Cato Vierra was granted a permit by the Board of Supervisors to operate the St. Paul's ferry across Elkhorn Slough. Unfortunately for Lezere, his subdivision plans failed to materialize. Until the late 1870s, Charles Moss' terminal facilities were successful as Moss Landing's storage and shipping facilities bustled. However, in that decade Southern Pacific extended its lines through the area, idling the wharves and warehouses of

Moss Landing—the shipping industry could not compete with the railroad. Moss was able to pull out his assets; he moved to San Francisco a wealthy man. In the early twentieth century Moss Landing would once again prosper as whaling and fishing became major industries there.

In 1863, Castroville, Monterey County's second oldest town, was founded by Juan B. Castro. Castro was the son of Monterey's first alcalde, Simeon Castro, and Governor Pico's sister, Maria Antonia Pico. Juan Castro inherited his father's estate, which included the Bolsa Nueva y Moro Cojo rancho upon which Castroville was founded. Castro subdivided his land to induce settlement, the first landowner to do so in Monterey County. Juan Pomber began the community's first grocery store. By 1865 Wells Fargo had established an office in Castroville and by 1866 a newspaper was published there. Two years later, owing to its favorable transportation location, the town had lumberyards, a flour mill, saloons, hotels, merchandise stores, a creamery considered one of the best in the state, and several other businesses. It would also boast one of the largest fruit-packing plants in the area. The county's first hospital was built and opened in Castroville in 1865, and in 1867 a post office was established. In the 1870s the town's chief industries were agricultural, with hay, grain, potatoes, sugar beets, and dairy products the main commodities produced.

Castro had donated a right-of-way through the Bolsa Nueva y Moro Cojo to the Southern Pacific Railroad, as well as donating land to SP for a depot in Castroville. Unfortunately for Castro and his new town, Southern Pacific chose Pajaro over Castroville as the location for their roundhouse operations. Salinas then boomed as the commercial center of the Salinas Valley and became what Castro had envisioned for his rancho.

In the southern part of the Salinas Valley, Soledad grew due to its location as the terminus, until 1886, of the railroad. All South County busi-

Facing page: When the Southern Pacific Railroad chose Pajaro over Castroville as the site for its major railroad facility, Castroville's hopes for becoming the Salinas Valley's major community faded. It remained a major transportation crossroad, however, as it does today. The general merchandise store in this photo can be seen in downtown Castroville, as that location still possesses some of its turn-of-the-century appearance. Courtesy, Denzil and Jennie Verardo

Above and below: Castroville was founded in 1863 by Juan B. Castro. It soon boasted numerous commercial buildings including a meat market, lumberyards, hotels, merchandise stores, and a number of saloons. At one time, Castroville had one of the area's largest fruit-packing plants, and in 1865 the county's first hospital operated in the town. Courtesy, Denzil and Jennie Verardo

ness had to be transacted there. At the turn of the century, hay, beets, and potatoes were the town's major commodities. On March 7, 1922, Soledad was incorporated with 550 residents.

In 1884 Charles H. King purchased 13,000 acres of Rancho San Lorenzo in order to plant grain. He had made his fortune in the redwood lumber industry in Eureka and was in a position to pay $105,000 for the land, which included the stock on it. King farmed 8,000 of his acres, which he had planted in wheat, and maintained 150 horses, which, along with the necessary equipment, allowed him to seed 100 acres of land daily.

In 1886 the Southern Pacific railroad extended its line to that area, and the value of King's land increased dramatically. C.H. King sold his holdings to the Spreckels Sugar Company in 1897. The arrival of SP also facilitated the founding of King City, and on July 11, 1886, Salinas merchant Judge William Vanderhurst opened the town's first store. The townsite was subdivided in 1887 and King City would soon boast a flour mill, a supply station for the mines, and a stage stop. King City incorporated in February 1911 as "The City of King."

In 1874 Chualar was laid out by David

Jacks on a portion of his ranch. The location had been named by padres for the large Indian rancheria that was located there. The railroad was responsible for Chualar's settlement attraction, and its first store was opened to handle supplies for railroad laborers. In the 1890s an influx of Danish settlers added to the town's ethnic diversity.

In 1836 Teodoro Gonzalez received a Mexican land grant in the central portion of the Salinas Valley. In 1872 the Gonzalez family deeded a 100-foot right-of-way through their rancho to the SP Railroad. Named after the family, the community of Gonzales was established in 1874 by Teodoro's sons, Mariano and Alfred, and by 1894 the town had a population of 500. In 1899, when Mariano and Alfred Gonzalez subdivided their land into 100-acre dairy farms, they left a legacy to the area that is evident to the present day. Italian-Swiss settlers brought improved dairy herds to the area and became prominent in the industry; in the next century, they would own 228 out of Monterey County's 1,891

Facing page, top: On October 25, 1877, Cato Vierra was granted a permit by the Board of Supervisors to operate a ferry across Elkhorn Slough. Supervisors set the ferry's tolls, which were: 25 cents for a saddle horse and man; $1 for a two-horse wagon; and $1.50 for a four-horse wagon. Increased traffic required the ferry to be replaced by the bridge seen here in 1890. Courtesy, Monterey County Historical Society

Facing page, middle: Moss Landing was an important commercial whaling center in the first two decades of the twentieth century. In 1919 the whaler Hercules landed a sperm whale one mile from Moss Landing. Whaling played an important role in the local economy until 1923, when demand for whale products dropped, and whales became increasingly scarce. Courtesy, Monterey County Historical Society

Facing page, bottom: Due to the periodic flooding and high winter water level which characterized the Salinas River, bridges were essential. In earlier times when fording the river was impractical, the west side of the Valley was cut off from the east. The King City Bridge #1, shown in this photo, later allowed access across the river from both directions. Photo by Lewis Slevin. Courtesy, Monterey County Library

Left: The "City of King" was incorporated in February 1911. However, King City had been the major commercial community in the southern Salinas Valley since the Southern Pacific Railroad extended its line to that area in 1886. Salinas merchant William Vanderhurst opened the city's first store, which was soon joined by many commercial enterprises. Courtesy, Monterey County Historical Society

Below: In 1911 occasional flooding would be so severe that some of the "modern" bridges across the Salinas River suffered damage. Thus, to continue mail service during these times, several "Flying Ducks," cable-drawn baskets which could be pulled back and forth across the river, were used to ensure delivery. Courtesy, Monterey County Library

Facing page: Paraiso Hot Springs, a resort known for its warm natural waters, lies above the Salinas Valley on the eastern slope of the Santa Lucia Mountains. Paraiso Springs was originally part of Mission Soledad, having been granted to the mission in 1791. The hot springs, which were used for healing the sick, were considered so healthful that they were named by the mission fathers Eternidad Paraiso, ("eternal paradise"). Photo by Lewis Slevin. Courtesy, Monterey County Library

farms. The establishment and success of Gonzales, as well as of Chualar, Soledad, and King City, are directly attributable to the extension of the railroad through the area.

Greenfield was not founded until after the turn of the century. Originally called Clark Colony, it was begun by real estate promoters in 1905. J.S. Clark was one of the organizers of the venture and lent his name to the new settlement. Twenty-acre parcels were sold to arriving settlers by the Arroyo Seco Improvement Company. These purchasers struggled in a futile attempt to farm the arid land. Fortunately, a canal was soon built to provide a consistent water supply to the area and the town of Greenfield became a viable agricul-

tural community, as its name implies—a tribute to the hardiness of the area's new settlers. By 1911 the town was a prosperous center for the Valley's fruit industry, and by 1914 its apples took first prize in the California Apple Show in San Francisco.

The Salinas Valley's growth was centered around its agricultural development, and within its various communities, politics reflected the Valley's agrarian economy. As the agricultural economics of the Valley changed, so too did its level of po-

litical activity. That activity reflected the Valley's rural, agricultural nature.

The election of 1856 gave the few Salinas Valley settlers who could vote an opportunity to cast their ballot for an individual they knew. John C. Fremont, who had traversed the area, ran as the Republican candidate for president of the United States. Unfortunately for Fremont, he polled a poor third place in California and lost the national election. However, he fared very well in Monterey County due to the familiarity of his ex-

ploits. In the crucial election of 1860, Abraham Lincoln carried only nine California counties, but Monterey County was one of them.

As the Salinas Valley's population increased, so did its political diversity. A depression occurred after the Panic of 1873 and industrial and gold production declined. During the same period, wheat dropped in price and sheep sold for as little as one dollar each. In 1873 the Salinas Grange of the Patrons of Husbandry organized to deal with the farmer's economic woes.

The Chinese, a source of cheap labor for California manufacturing, railroads, and mines, were unjustly seen as a cause of the state's economic ills. Thus it was no surprise that valley residents banded together to support anti-Chinese

measures, as did other communities across California.

In 1877 in San Francisco, the Workingmen's Party of California was formed uniting various anti-Chinese organizations, as well as those individuals impacted most heavily by the oppressive economic conditions, such as farmers and ranchers. In January 1878 a state convention of the Workingmen's Party met in San Francisco, and the party began to pick up support. By March 1878 a Salinas Workingmen's branch was formed supporting the statewide organization.

California created a new constitution in 1879 with several concessions made to the Workingmen's Party, which had by then developed into a considerable political force. During the ratification process, urban counties such as Alameda and San Francisco rejected it, but the agricultural Salinas Valley voted heavily for its ratification. The constitution was approved by a narrow margin. While never reaching the level of support the Republicans and Democrats enjoyed, the Working-

men nevertheless influenced both major parties. Political success in the Valley meant dealing effectively with the area's agrarian characteristics and agricultural economy.

It was the city of Salinas which was destined to become the political, economic, and population center of the Valley.

Facing page, top: While the twentieth century brought major social, economic, and demographic changes to the Salinas Valley, some of the area's communities did remain relatively unaltered. This 1930 photograph shows Jolon looking much the same as it did in the nineteenth century. The notable change is that the automobile replaced the horse. Jolon today serves as a resting place for the traveler journeying to and from the Hunter Liggett Military Reservation. Courtesy, Monterey County Library

Facing page, bottom and below: The salt ponds of Moss Landing have long been well-known landmarks. Initially, the salt ponds were constructed in the late nineteenth century by the Vierra family, and soon became an important and successful commercial enterprise. The Monterey Bay Salt Works plant and salt ponds are seen here in operation in 1919. Photo by Lewis Slevin. Courtesy, Monterey County Library

CHAPTER THREE

A True American City

Salinas is a central place for business for the whole valley, and directly on the line of the great southern railroad . . . It has all those facilities for the arts, sciences, conveniences, and benefits connected with such a place. Its county buildings, churches, schools, hotels, stores, shops and residences cause it to rank among the first of its size in the State. The town is embowered in trees and adorned with pleasant gardens and lovely flowers. The aspect of the whole is that of a true, enterprising, progressive, permanent American city.

—History of Monterey County, *1881*

Children's activities were officially added to Big Week in 1930 with a Kiddie Kaper parade featuring local children in costume, as a prelude to the Como del Rodeo parade. Courtesy, Monterey County Historical Society

At the turn of the century, blacksmith shops like this one in Salinas were called upon not only to shoe horses and repair carriages, but also to manufacture the agricultural implements that area farmers needed. Courtesy, Denzil and Jennie Verardo

When this description appeared in the 1881 Elliott and Moore *History of Monterey County*, Salinas was a seven-year-old city with approximately 2,000 residents. Even then, its destiny to become the leading community in the Salinas Valley seemed assured. The idea that the location of the future county seat might be attributed to an accident seems to have had little detrimental effect on its progress and development.

According to local lore, in 1856 Deacon Elias Howe had his wagonload of lumber shift and dump out onto the ground. He decided to build his building where it lay instead of reloading it. It is known that Howe purchased property from Jacob P. Leese at the crossroads of the Monterey-San Juan Bautista and Watsonville-Los Angeles routes. There, accidentally or by design, he built a stagecoach stop which he named Halfway House, and Salinas had its start. Howe's Half-

way House was so successful that stagecoach activities shifted there from Natividad, spelling doom for the latter community.

Howe operated his establishment for nine years, and then sold it to Albert Trescony for $800. By this time the settlement had achieved some sense of permanence with the establishment of a post office in the Halfway House in 1864. Trescony's involvement here was relatively short-lived. In 1868 he sold the Halfway House to Alanson Riker and William Jackson and moved to the South Valley, where he became a successful rancher.

The new owners felt that the area had great potential to become a prosperous community, and with the cooperation and generosity of wealthy landowner Eugene Sherwood, they proposed to lay out a city. The Riker-Jackson property adjoined the Sherwood tract, separated only by a fence. Removing that barrier, they laid out a half-mile-square townsite, the center of which would become the intersection of Main and Gabilan Streets. On March 1, 1868, town lots ranging in price from $100 to $1,000 were offered for sale to the public. In less than two months, the settlement's few original buildings were joined by numerous business establishments including 27 saloons in full operation. A school was soon opened in an old saloon on the west side of Main Street with Sophronia Harvey (the wife of Nathan Clark) as its first teacher. The foresight of the merchant Riker and the philanthropist Sherwood seemed to have been rewarded with some haste.

Families whose names would be memorialized on city streets and buildings began arriving and assisting in the development of the new community. James B. Iverson opened a blacksmith shop on Gabilan Street and was soon meeting the additional need for agricultural implements. As his enterprise prospered, Iverson's brother was able to come from Denmark and the partnership that eventually resulted was known as Iverson Brothers. Michael Hughes moved his harness shop from Monterey and was joined by J.V. Lacy, whose blacksmith shop had also previously been located in the seaside community.

James Jeffrey soon opened the town's first restaurant and eventually expanded his business enterprise into the Jeffrey House. Carlisle S. Abbott, who had arrived in the area with the 500 dairy cattle he had driven down from Marin County, built the first brick hotel, the Abbott House, in 1874. These hotels, together with Michael Tynan's Diamond, Salinas, and Commercial hotels, provided ample accommodations for the visitor.

Samuel Geil and Judge John K. Alexander

In 1890 Carlisle S. Abbott was one of Salinas' leading men. In addition to his large ranching interests, he also built the Abbott House, was president of the Monterey and Salinas Valley Railroad, and represented the area in the state legislature. Courtesy, Monterey County Library

Above: In June 1878 the first telephone connection was made between the telegraph office in the Abbott House, Salinas, and the Southern Pacific Depot. Nine years later the telephone company was petitioned to extend service past midnight. Meeting the growing demand for communications kept Salinas switchboard operators busy. Courtesy, Monterey County Historical Society

came to practice law, while J.H. McDougall acted both as banker and early postmaster. Conklin & Samuels and Vanderhurst & Sanborn joined Riker as Salinas merchants. W.P.L. Winham moved his business to town in 1868, becoming one of Salinas' early real estate agents.

The influx and influence of Americans in the area had begun long before the official founding of Salinas, though. Several months before California became a state, the legislature had created Monterey County as one of the original 27. At that time, February 1850, the county seat was located at Monterey and the population of the entire county totaled less than 2,000. Cattle was the major economic resource and would continue to be for another decade. But in 1852, James Bryant Hill began to sow the seeds of change when he planted 95 acres of barley on the Salinas plain. Two years later Hill had fenced in more than 400 acres and was preparing to enclose more. He had also begun the community of Hilltown, establishing a post office there in 1854. And, although the post office was moved to Salinas a decade later, Hilltown retained its importance as a ferry crossing on the Salinas River, connecting Salinas and Monterey.

From J.B. Hill's modest beginnings, grain production increased dramatically. In 1866 the Pacific Coast Steamship Company opened a terminal for handling grain bound from Monterey to San Francisco. This was supplemented by Captain Moss' landing near Elkhorn Slough.

The most important factor in the expansion of grain production occurred in 1872, though, when the Southern Pacific Railroad extended its line down from San Francisco to Salinas. Ignoring pleas from the settlements of Santa Rita, Blanco, and Hilltown, the railroad company decided to go through the middle of the Valley straight to Salinas. The impact of that decision is still obvious today. Salinas became the railhead—the terminus for wagon freight—and its importance as such precipitated two drastic changes for the community. On September 17, 1872, the Monterey County Supervisors declared Salinas an incorporated city. The incorporation move-

Facing page, top: The growing city of Salinas depended on the mail for most of its communication with the rest of the country and the world. At the time of this photo, 1904, the population of the city had surpassed 3,000. Courtesy, Denzil and Jennie Verardo

Facing page, bottom: One of the largest mills in the state, the Sperry Flour Mill on New Street in Salinas had a daily capacity of 500 barrels. Its Drifted Snow Flour was renowned, as was the Salinas Valley wheat which supplied it. Courtesy, Monterey County Historical Society

ment, which was backed by a petition signed by 112 of the 140 qualified voters of Salinas, had involved several key figures, including William Vanderhurst, Judge Alexander, Carlisle Abbott, and S. McConnell Shearer.

In addition to the city status granted to Salinas, the supervisors ordered an election in November of that year to decide whether to move the county seat from Monterey.

There were two strong proponents of moving the county seat to Salinas—the communities of Salinas and Hollister. At the time, the San Benito area was part of Monterey County, and residents of the growing community of Hollister objected to the long and often difficult journey to the county seat at Monterey to conduct their business. What they actually desired was the creation of a new county with Hollister as its seat of government. In exchange for support from Salinas for the creation of San Benito County, voters in Hollister played the pivotal role in the relocation of Monterey County's center of government.

The campaign was intense, with Natividad, Santa Rita, and Castroville eventually abandoning their own individual bids in favor of Monterey. Local stories told of campaign "war chests" developed by both sides. One even credits the outcome of the election to a poker game in which the Salinas group was able to sufficiently deflate the treasury of the Monterey group to render it defenseless.

When the ballots were counted, Salinas was the new county seat, thus virtually assuring the break-off of the San Benito area from Monterey County.

The state legislature, among whose members was Assemblyman Carlisle Abbott, voted to create San Benito County and on February 12, 1874, Governor Booth signed the bill. At that point, Monterey County lost about one-third of its land, population, and tax revenue.

Less than one month later, on March 4, 1874, Salinas was made a chartered city by a

The Great Earthquake of April 18, 1906, had a major impact on the Salinas Valley. Roads like this one became impassable, railroad tracks were twisted, and many buildings suffered damage. Courtesy, Denzil and Jennie Verardo

special act of the legislature. An election was then held and Isaac Julian Harvey became the first mayor of Salinas. He was joined by councilmen Burbeck Hughes, J.B. Iverson, Dr. Tuttle, William Vanderhurst, and William Willcoxen. The population of Salinas had reached 700 and its steady expansion appeared ready to burst into a boom.

Salinas was described a short time later as "the most prosperous and thriving city of its size in the State of California . . . It is progressive and rapidly increasing in population, while its manufacturing interests show a healthy and satisfactory growth." In response to the new abundance of wheat, the Salinas Flouring Mill Company built one of the largest mills in the state here in 1883. It would later be known as the Central Milling Company's Salinas Mill, and then as the Sperry Flour Mill it would gain fame with its production of "Drifted Snow" flour.

J.H. Menke constructed the Salinas Brewery in partnership with Mr. Lurz. Its celebrated "Schloss Brau" was distributed throughout the Central Coast of California and its impact on the city's economy was felt well into the twentieth century.

Frederick A. Hihn, one of the leading businessmen of Santa Cruz County, operated the Salinas

Planing Mill here, and Salinas could boast of several dry goods, clothing, and grocery stores, hotels, banks, tailors, photographers, a saddlery, meat markets, blacksmiths, two flour mills, a brewery, lawyers, doctors, and merchants of many varieties, and five cigar factories.

After the courthouse in Salinas burned in January 1877, there was talk of moving the county seat back to Monterey. To prevent that eventuality, Jesse D. Carr provided a site for a new county building on West Alisal Street for one dollar. The site is still being used today. Carr, whose involvement with the development of Salinas spanned two centuries, has been memorialized in Carr Lake, a 1,475-acre area northeast of downtown Salinas that he drained and reclaimed. After arriving in California during the

The San Francisco Earthquake of 1906 destroyed the Ford and Sanborn Store, shown here, as well as damaged every business in town. Windows were broken and merchandise scattered, and half of the homes in Salinas lost their chimneys. The rear wall of the Abbott House also collapsed. Courtesy, Monterey County Historical Society

Gold Rush, Carr eventually became one of the largest landowners in Monterey County. But his impact was felt well beyond the county lines. An influential conservative Democrat who was often mentioned as a potential governor or senator, Jesse Carr served as president of the State Board of Agriculture and as a member of the University of California Board of Regents. He was also a guest at President Cleveland's inaugurations in 1885 and 1893. He was credited with owning "the finest private residence in Salinas."

Just as business was developing and prospering in the infant city, agriculture was expanding and adding its share to the ever-improving economy of the area. Dairying increased and the Salinas Creamery Company's "Golden Rod" butter soon developed a reputation for outstanding quality. By 1902 the area's Salinas Burbank potatoes

Local Troop C of the National Guard was called out to assist residents following the 1906 San Francisco Earthquake. Salinas skies "glowed like copper" for many nights during the resulting fires 110 miles to the north. Courtesy, Monterey County Historical Society

had developed a reputation for being without equal. *The Resources of California* reported that "As high as four hundred bushels to the acre were raised near Salinas." Markets for the Burbanks extended from the northwestern United States to the Philippine Islands. The significance of the potato to Salinas may be best illustrated by the fact that in 1911, instead of selecting a queen for its first rodeo, Salinas chose instead to have the event presided over by "King Spud."

As important as Burbank potatoes were to the Salinas area, it was another agricultural crop whose processing precipitated the establishment of the area's first major industrial facility. In the

1850s Claus Spreckels had come to California after making a sizeable fortune in the grocery business in South Carolina. Upon arriving in San Francisco, Spreckels again invested in grocery stores. These proved lucrative enough to allow his investment in other businesses as well as in the purchase of an estate and resort in Aptos in Santa Cruz County.

Claus Spreckels also developed an interest in sugar refining, and in 1865 he returned to his native Germany to explore the possibilities of refining beet sugar. He conducted this research by working as a common laborer in a German sugar beet mill. Returning to the West Coast, Spreckels organized the California Sugar Refinery, but because it was not yet practical or economical to use sugar beets, he imported cane from the Philippines, China, Java, and Hawaii.

Claus Spreckels had also established very close ties with Hawaiian King Kalakaua, and eventually he controlled such a significant portion of Hawaii's cane plantations that he became known as the "Sugar King of Hawaii." Political tides turned, however, and by 1886 Spreckels was facing open hostility from restive native growers. At that point, he felt it was time to turn to sugar beets.

Top: Early sugar beet production was labor intensive and many Chinese workers were utilized topping the beets in the fields before transport to the refinery. Beets were topped manually until the advent of the Marbeet Harvester in the 1940s. Courtesy, Monterey County Historical Society

Above: The main building of the Spreckels Sugar Refinery near Salinas was damaged in the 1906 San Francisco Earthquake, although the extent of the damage appeared exaggerated because some repairs were already in progress when the earthquake struck. Courtesy, Monterey County Historical Society

Mule and horse-drawn wagons were used to transport sugar beets to waiting freight trains for the trip to the Spreckels refinery. This was the King City depot during the first season in the Salinas Valley in 1899. Courtesy, Monterey County Historical Society

In exchange for commitments from local growers to plant and grow at least 2,000 acres of sugar beets each year and for the community's donation of land for a factory site, Spreckels agreed to construct his beet sugar refinery in Watsonville. When completed in 1888, the factory, which could process 1,000 tons of beets per day, promised great prosperity for Watsonville and the Pajaro Valley.

Demand for sugar necessitated expansion of both the Watsonville factory itself and the acreage planted to beets. Within eight years, Claus Spreckels was seeking a new factory site in a location that could provide more beet growing land than could the Pajaro Valley. He didn't have to look far.

By September 1899 Spreckels began operations at his new facility, then the world's largest

sugar refinery, about four miles south of Salinas. The factory's main building was five stories high, 582 feet long, and 102 feet wide. It alone contained 3,500 tons of steel, 4 million bricks, and 800 squares of slate. The plant could process 3,000 tons of beets per day, creating some 450 pounds of raw sugar. During its first year in operation, the plant, with its more than 300 employees working around the clock and seven days a week during the season or "campaign," produced 38,437,300 pounds of sugar.

Much as some Salinas Valley growers had supplied the Watsonville refinery, Pajaro Valley beet growers shipped their crop to the new plant. And, although the narrow-gage Pajaro Valley Railroad provided a fairly economical means of transportation between Watsonville and Spreckels, the major portion of the beets was grown in the Salinas Valley. In addition to the development of a new and profitable crop for the area, the success of the Spreckels Sugar Company factory also resulted in the establishment of a new community.

As soon as Claus Spreckels had completed his Salinas Valley refinery in 1898, he set about to build an adjacent town. The first town building was the Spreckels Hotel, which was intended to house the factory's workers. In order to meet the need for additional housing, especially for families, Spreckels had houses erected (or in some cases moved in) nearby. The company then built a store and would later add on a second story to it to provide the community with a dance hall. A school was soon constructed, a volunteer fire company organized, and the community of Spreckels became a thriving town.

Other businesses joined the Spreckels Sugar Company, and soon after the turn of the century, Spreckels had a meat market; livery; grocery; clothing store; lumberyard; cabinet, plumbing, and bicycle shops; a laundry; a barber; doctors; and its own bank. The Bank of Spreckels, begun in 1907 by D.W. McLeod, was disincorporated in 1912, but it did handle all of the company's local banking and served the town's needs for its five years of existence.

Spreckels also had a saloon, the Louvre, which not only kept the town's thirst quenched but also seemed to keep a large portion of the factory workers' paychecks. In 1912 women of the community successfully circulated an anti-saloon petition, and on September 13 of that year, when all of the town's liquor licenses expired, Spreckels became "dry."

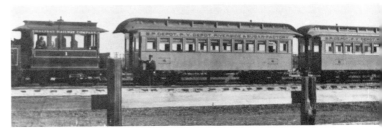

Above: The Salinas Railway Company, which had been established to meet the need for passenger service between the town of Spreckels and Salinas, used this "Dinky" which had operated previously on California Street in San Francisco to carry passengers to and from the Cliff House and Sutro Baths. Courtesy, Monterey County Historical Society

Below: Salinas Cavalry Troop C, which had been organized in August 1895, is shown here marching from the armory on West Alisal Street (building with flag) to the train depot on its way to fight Pancho Villa at the Mexican border in 1914. Courtesy, Monterey County Historical Society

Although wheat, potatoes, sugar beets, and eventually row crops replaced a great deal of the ranching activity in the Valley by the early 1900s, there remained a significant involvement with livestock raising and competition. In the late 1800s, Eugene Sherwood deeded more than 50 acres on the northern edge of Salinas to the city to be used as a park and for an annual fair. A horse-racing track was developed and it became known

Top: In the early 1900s the 300 block of Main Street in Salinas was known as the Garage Center because of its many automobile dealerships. Courtesy, Denzil and Jennie Verardo

Above: It became a Big Week tradition for everyone in Salinas to wear Western cowboy outfits, and bankers were no exception. For many years anyone appearing on Main Street without Western attire was "locked-up" in the "hoosegow" constructed for Big Week spoilsports. Courtesy, Denzil and Jennie Verardo

not only for its competitions but also as a breeding area for prize mares and studs.

Then on August 1, 1911, an event was begun as a sideshow to the races which would eventually not only replace the horse races but would give the Salinas Valley another worldwide claim to fame. A 1936 *Salinas Californian* article described the rodeo's beginnings:

Seeking an added attraction for the program of horse races held here annually at Sherwood's Park by the Pacific Coast Trotting Horse Breeders Association, a group of Salinas and Southern Monterey County leaders conceived the idea of staging the western show in the infield of the race track to keep the cash customers from becoming bored with waits between races.

In 1913 the event's organizers incorporated as the California Rodeo with J.R. Hebbron as president. Early shows attracted such distinguished guests as Senator James D. Phelan, Mayor "Sunny Jim" Rolph of San Francisco, Major General Leonard Wood, and Secretary of War Lindley Garrison. Another visitor, famous race-car driver Barney Oldfield, managed not only to see the rodeo, but to get a speeding ticket near Santa Rita.

Salinas soon developed a "Big Week" around the rodeo. To kick off rodeo activities, the first "Big Hat" barbecue was held in 1913, and has since become the traditional start of the annual rodeo. "King Spud" was the rodeo's first royalty in 1911 and was replaced eventually by both a Rodeo Queen and Rodeo Sweetheart. A Saturday night parade, known as the "Comado del Rodeo" and later as the "Como del Rodeo," originated in 1913, as did the daily horse parades down Main Street to the park.

In 1925 a new $40,000 grandstand that seated 10,000 was built at Sherwood Park, and in 1930 a Kiddie Kapers parade was added to the festivities. Salinas became known as the "Home of the California Rodeo."

Meanwhile in some nearby fields, another agricultural development was beginning to take shape which would not only bestow new titles on the city, but would assure growth and prosperity for many decades. In 1914 Moses S. Hutchings planted three acres of lettuce on land in the Pajaro Valley. His experiment succeeded astoundingly well. Within a few years, hundreds of railroad cars of lettuce were being shipped annually from Watsonville.

Orrin O. Eaton is credited with having planted the first lettuce in Monterey County in 1917. A few others, like the Bardins and Vierras, also tried small acreages of the new crop. Then in 1922, the California Vegetable Union tried to interest Salinas Valley farmers in the potential in growing lettuce. E.W. Palmtag, director of the Salinas Chamber of Commerce, was an ardent supporter of the venture, as was the chamber, and was successful in convincing a number of growers to participate. The volunteers, mostly from the Blanco district, agreed to plant a total of 350 acres in lettuce that year. Only 175 acres were actually planted and only a small percentage of that was harvested due to the unfamiliarity of the farmers with the crop. But the lettuce industry was begun nevertheless and Salinas would never be the same afterwards.

Below: Civic pride in the young city was demonstrated by activities such as this Arbor Day gathering in March 1916 in Central Park. In addition to fine parks, Salinas residents could also avail themselves of cultural presentations in one of the city's theaters or the opera house. Courtesy, Monterey County Library

Above: One of the impressive events of Big Week has been the daily horse parade down Main Street to the rodeo grounds. In 1912 the streets were decorated with oriental lanterns for Big Week festivities. Courtesy, Monterey County Historical Society

John Steinbeck
The Long Valley's Most Famous Son

Please feel free to make up your own facts about me as you need them. I can't remember how much of me really happened and how much I invented.

Such was one reply credited to Nobel Prize-winning author John Steinbeck when asked for biographical information.

John Ernst Steinbeck was born in Salinas on February 27, 1902. His father, John Ernst Steinbeck, who had moved several times in his young life, had settled in King City, where he managed the flour mill and met and eventually married a young teacher, Olive Hamilton. In 1894 the family, which by then included two daughters, moved to Salinas. Steinbeck went to work managing the Sperry Flour Mill on Castroville Street. John, the third Steinbeck child and only son, was born in their large Victorian family home on Central Avenue. Another daughter was born a few years later and it seems the family led a happy and stable life. Both Olive and John Ernst were well educated and encouraged learning and cultural growth in their children. By all accounts, young John seems to have gotten into a fairly normal amount of boyish trouble, usually acting as an instigator and leader among his friends.

In 1915 John Steinbeck entered Salinas High School as part of a class of 28 freshmen. He

was a good, though not great, student, and based on his popularity, grades, and performance in athletics he was chosen senior class president. He was also selected to be associate editor of *El Gavilan*, the school newspaper, further fueling his quiet ambition to become a writer.

Steinbeck entered Stanford University as a journalism major in October 1919. His first year at the university did not produce the success that he had found in high school, and by late fall of his sophomore year, a dean's warning about his poor grades prompted him to leave Stanford. At first hesitant to return to Salinas and face the parents he felt he had let down, Steinbeck worked in the Bay Area and then on a ranch in South County. After finally returning home in 1922, he found work at the Spreck-

els Sugar Refinery as a chemist.

Steinbeck was determined to return to Stanford and succeeded in doing so in January 1923. Although he was much more successful academically on this try, he left Stanford in 1925 without a degree or a job prospect but with a determined commitment to write.

After working unsuccessfully to complete a manuscript he started at Stanford, Steinbeck went by freighter to New York, where he spent two years working at jobs ranging from newspaper reporting to bricklaying at the new Madison Square Garden. He was still unable to sell his manuscripts and returned to California, taking a job as a caretaker and then as a fish sorter near Lake Tahoe. While there, he completed *Cup of Gold*, which was to be his first published book. A year after its 1929 publication, John Steinbeck married Carol Henning. They moved into the family's Pacific Grove cottage, where they could live rent-free, and Carol worked as a secretary and typist to support them and allow John to write.

It was during this period that Steinbeck established one of the most important relationships of his life—his friendship with Edward Ricketts. Ricketts, a marine biologist and owner of the Pacific Biological Laboratory on Monterey's Cannery Row, would be immortalized by his younger friend as "Doc" in *Cannery Row* (1945) and *Sweet Thursday* (1954).

During the Great Depression period, Steinbeck drew on many Salinas Valley experiences to create *The Pastures of Heaven* (1932); *To a God Unknown* (1933); *Tortilla Flat* (1935); *In Dubious Battle* (1936); *Of Mice and Men* (1937); *The Red Pony* (1937); and a stage version of *Of Mice and Men*, which appeared on Broadway in 1937 and won the Drama Critics Circle Award. *Tortilla Flat* became a bestseller, and that, along with the success of *In Dubious Battle*, afforded John Steinbeck financial independence and the new luxury of travel. The Steinbecks went to Europe in 1937, again by freighter, and upon their return in 1938, *The Long Valley*, a collection of short stories, was published.

The Grapes of Wrath, Steinbeck's greatest work and certainly one of his most controversial in the Salinas Valley, was published in 1939. It earned Steinbeck a Pulitzer Prize in 1940 and membership in the National Institute of Arts and Letters, as well as substantial royalty income. But this novel, together with articles he had done on migrant labor conditions in 1936 for the *San Francisco News*, and accounts he wrote for *Life* magazine and *The Nation* attacking the deplorable living conditions of migrant farm workers, earned him a reputation as a muckraker, and a level of despisement in his hometown.

Following a scientific expedition with Ed Ricketts to the Gulf of California, Steinbeck collaborated with his friend on a log of the journey which was published in 1941 as the *Sea of Cortez*.

John Steinbeck was almost 40 when the United States entered World War II, and although he was too old for active military duty, he chose to make his contribution by writing *Bombs Away* (1942). Not only was this work an effective recruiting tool for the Air Force, but it was purchased by a motion picture company and the royalties went to the military. The success of *Bombs Away* did not quench Steinbeck's thirst for involvement in the war effort, however, and in 1943 he went to the Mediterranean as a *New York Herald Tribune* correspondent.

Steinbeck was divorced from Carol in 1942, and married entertainer Gwyndolyn Conger in March 1943. They tried to settle in nearby Monterey, but as Steinbeck wrote to a friend in 1945, "I hate the feeling of persecution, but I am just not welcome here . . . This isn't my country anymore. And it won't be until I am dead. It makes me very sad." They moved to New York, where Steinbeck worked to create *Cannery Row* (1945), *The Pearl* (1947), *The Wayward Bus* (1947), and *A Russian Journal* with photographer Robert Capa in 1948. The marriage produced two sons, although by 1948 Steinbeck was again divorced.

That same year, Ed Ricketts died as a result of an automobile-train accident, and, faced with the failure of his second marriage and the loss of his dear friend, John Steinbeck seemed to throw himself into his writing. With the support of his third wife Elaine Scott, whom he had married in 1950, the prodigious au-

thor published *The Log of the Sea of Cortez* (1951) which included a profile of Ed Ricketts; *East of Eden* (1952); *Sweet Thursday* (1954); *The Short Reign of Pippin IV* (1957); and *The Winter of Our Discontent* (1961).

In 1962 John Steinbeck was awarded the Nobel Prize for Literature. Two years later he was presented with the U.S. Medal of Freedom. He also published *Travels with Charley in Search of America* (1962) and *America and Americans* (1966), both reflective of his renewed love of his country and its people.

Steinbeck received many other honors, including the Press Medal of Freedom, trusteeship of the John F. Kennedy Memorial Library, and membership in the National Arts Council. Eventually the new Salinas Public Library was named for him. His brilliant writing made him one of the greatest American novelists. He had the ability to turn even commonplace activities into incredibly insightful experiences and he genuinely loved and cared about people. He gave the world an impressive and expressive look at the Salinas Valley with all of its beauty, and with its rough spots. He earned the Nobel Prize for "his realistic as well as imaginative writings, distinguished by sympathetic humor and a keen social perception."

On December 20, 1968, John Steinbeck died in his New York home. His ashes were returned to Salinas and placed in the Hamilton family plot in the Garden of Memories. The Long Valley's most famous son was finally welcomed home.

CHAPTER FOUR

Steinbeck's Legacy

*Salinas was never a pretty town. It took a
darkness from the swamps. The high gray
fog hung over it and the ceaseless wind
blew up the valley, cold and with a kind
of desolate monotony. The mountains on
both sides of the valley were beautiful, but
Salinas was not and we knew it. Perhaps
that is why a kind of violent assertiveness,
an energy like the compensation for sin
grew up in the town. The town motto . . .
was "Salinas is."*

—*John Steinbeck,* Holiday Magazine, *June 1955*

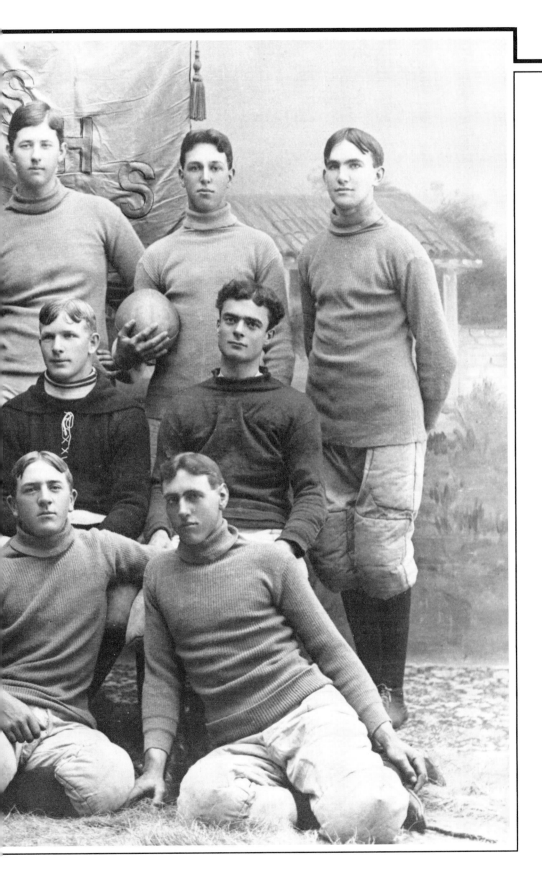

Even in 1897, high school life was not limited to academics. This Salinas High School football team appears ready to defend the school's athletic honor. Courtesy, Monterey County Historical Society

*The office of the Salinas City Index was busy
even at the turn of the century, when most of the printing process was accomplished by hand. The two gentle-
men wielding pad and pen are probably reporters
posed for the photograph. Courtesy, Denzil and
Jennie Verardo*

The task of defining for a community, and for the
rest of the world, what it is and what it was, has
long been carried out by local newspapers. And
the Salinas Valley has been fortunate in having
journalistic enterprises in almost all of its settlements. From the *King City Settler,* which has
been replaced by the *King City Rustler,* to the *Greenfield News, Soledad Bee, Gonzales Tribune,* and the
Castroville Times and *Argus,* the Valley has had
sources of international, national, and perhaps
more importantly, local news.

In the city of Salinas, the decade of the
1870s saw the establishment of two local news-

papers, the *Salinas Democrat* and the *Salinas City Index.* The *Democrat* had originally been founded
in Monterey in 1867 as the *Monterey Democrat,*
but its editor J.W. Leigh moved it to Salinas in
1872, shortly before the county seat was shifted
there. In the late 1880s one of the *Democrat's*
new owners, Thomas Harris, entered into a partnership with M.J. Smeltzer; in 1889 they launched
the *Salinas Daily Journal.* The two papers were
later merged, with the *Democrat* becoming the
weekly edition of the *Journal* and dropping its former name.

The *Index,* founded in 1871 by Melville By-
erly as the *Salinas City Weekly Index,* took over for Salinas' first newspaper, the *Salinas Valley Standard.*
The *Standard,* which was started in 1869 by
J. Selwyn Britain, survived for only a short time
after its sale to H.V. Morehouse, who moved it to
Santa Rita in 1871. Byerly's *Index* organization originally included George Clevenger, who left the

paper in 1874 to establish the *Monterey Herald* with his brother Stephen. Melville Byerly died in 1876 and the *Index* was soon sold to W. J. Hill.

W. J. "Old" Hill, who had earned that title during the 1860s while operating a ferry and fending off Indian attacks in Idaho, came to Salinas from Silver City, Idaho, where he had published that state's first newspaper, *The Avalanche*. Hill, who was described in Elliott and Moore's *History of Monterey County* as a "strong Republican," owned the *Index* for 33 years, and in the meantime served as a state senator and as mayor of Salinas. During Hill's tenure as editor and publisher, the *Salinas Index* was noted as "one of the leading interior journals of the State." In 1909 Hill sold the newspaper to the Salinas Index Publishing Company, composed of D.A. Madiera, F.H. Lang, H.E. Abbott, Frank Griffin, and Duncan Sterling. Fred Weybret purchased the *Index* from that company in 1919. Weybret then secured ownership of the *Salinas Daily Journal* from Paul P. Parker in July 1928 and consolidated the two

papers as the *Salinas Index-Journal*. Meanwhile, a daily evening paper, *The Owl*, had been established in Salinas in 1894 by H.L. Bradford. Though popular, it was to have a fairly short life.

In 1929 the weekly *Monterey County Post* was started by Marvin Londahl in Salinas. It was merged with the *Index-Journal* in 1936. On July 1, 1942, Salinas' newspapers were consolidated into the daily *Salinas Californian* by new owner Merritt Speidel and his Salinas Newspapers Inc. The *Californian* continues as the major daily newspaper in the Salinas Valley and is now a part of the Gannett newspaper chain.

Though much of the Valley's literary tradition can be traced directly to journalism, the

Whether delivered from the State Printing Office by freight wagon, or from the county library by the librarian, Anne Hadden, on horseback, the arrival of new books was an exciting event for many rural schoolchildren in the Salinas Valley. Courtesy, Monterey County Library

*Carrying out a distinctly patriotic theme, the
1916 Joint Commencement Exercises for the schools
in north Monterey County demonstrated support
both for public schools and for the country at the
onset of World War I. Courtesy, Monterey County
Library*

area did play host to one of the most renowned writers of the late nineteenth and early twentieth centuries, Gertrude Atherton. After marriage to George Atherton, her mother's suitor and son of wealthy San Francisco businessman Faxton Atherton, she spent time in the southern Salinas Valley while her husband managed the family's Rancho Milpitas. Some of her experiences during the 1877 stay were quite vividly and a bit caustically described in her autobiography, *Adventures of a Novelist.*

Another of the Valley's prominent literary women was Edith Margaret Coulter. Born in Salinas in 1880, she went on to write both about California history and librarianship. Coulter was a full professor at the University of California School of Librarianship at Berkeley when she retired in 1949.

Edith Coulter had come from an area with a long tradition of support for public library facilities. Harrison's 1889 descriptive history of Monterey County cited a new "$5000 free circulating library, a gift from the Hon. Jesse D. Carr," which was established in the IOOF Building on Main Street in Salinas. By 1909, assisted again by Jesse Carr, the Women's Civic Club of Salinas had secured a Carnegie Library for the city. The organization itself purchased the lot upon which the library was built at the corner of Main and San Luis streets. The collection from the IOOF library was combined with that of the Women's Christian Temperance Union, which had opened a reading room and book lending library in the 1890s, and placed in the handsome new building which was to serve the city until 1960.

In his 1881 *History of Monterey County*, Elliott described another Valley library, Castroville's, as a "public reading room, opened . . . by the local lodge of Good Templars . . . well supplied with books, magazines, and newspapers, most of them donated by members of the order . . . who have thus shown an interest in the success of an institution whose influence in behalf of education and good morals is bound to be felt in the community."

In 1913 the City Council of King City established a free public library in a room in City Hall with Mr. Catchpole as the first librarian. Two years later the King City Library became part of the County Library System.

The Board of Supervisors had established the Monterey County Free Library in August 1912, with Anne Hadden as its first librarian. Hadden was to gain some notoriety for her unique method of providing library services to remote areas of the county. She and a teacher companion would travel by train from Salinas to King City, having sent the books ahead by pack animal. At King City they would catch an auto stage for the trip to Jolon. Traveling from Jolon by horseback, they visited isolated settlements and families on both sides of the Santa Lucia Mountains, providing a contact point to the outside world with the books carried in their saddlebags. She then traveled back north to Salinas along the rugged Big Sur coastline. Hadden seems to have been the perfect choice for the job that she considered "a really wonderful library adventure."

In 1914 branches of the County Library were operating in Greenfield; Bradley, at the hotel; Cholame, in the school but later moved to Parkfield; and Castroville, in Mr. Witcher's store; as well as in Carmel, Aromas, Big Sur, and later at the Asilomar Conference Grounds.

From a library with no books in 1912, the County Library grew to have holdings of more than 590,000 books by 1980. Permanent library facilities have been established in the Salinas Valley at Bradley, Castroville, Gonzales, Greenfield, Pajaro, Parkfield, Prunedale, San Ardo, San Lucas, and Soledad, and a bookmobile, following Anne Hadden's example, serves remote areas of the county. The system is managed from library headquarters in Salinas, and while books now go out by van instead of by horseback, the County Library remains an important link to the outside world for much of the Salinas Valley.

In the 1880s the *Salinas Index* declared that,

Above and top: As the population of communities increased, so did the need for larger schools. With the arrival of the Southern Pacific Railroad, Soledad was assured of both growth and prosperity, as reflected in the expansion and modernization of its public schools. Courtesy, Pat Hathaway Photographs

concerning public schools, "outside of San Francisco, there are only a very few counties that can give a better account of themselves than Monterey, and those few have far greater wealth and population." At that time, about 2,400 of the 3,400 school-age children of the area were attending school in one of the more than 30 school districts in the Salinas Valley. In the 1980s, 100 years later, the 21 public school districts operating in the Valley serve more than 43,500 students from kindergarten through community college.

It is the Valley's community college that traces its roots back the farthest, although its historic ties appeared to have been severed on more than one occasion. In 1833 William Edward Petty Hartnell, landowner and citizen of the Salinas Valley, established "El Colegio de San Jose" in an adobe building near his home on Rancho Alisal. Hartnell sought to fill the need felt by wealthy local rancheros for improved educational advantages for their sons. For a year, a dozen or so students were taught

by Hartnell. But the lack of sufficient attendance made the school unprofitable and it was closed.

In 1920, 86 years later, the Board of Trustees of the Salinas High School District was authorized by the State to start a junior college. The Valley again had an institution of higher learning. Unfortunately, the college was to meet the same fate as Hartnell's "Colegio" when it was forced to close for a lack of students. By 1927 it was reopened with 35 students in two rooms on the Main Street side of the boys' gym at Salinas High School. The year 1929 saw the college's

Though this late nineteenth century chemistry lab at Salinas High School may now seem elementary and barely supplied, it did expose students to the experimental process. Some students of Salinas High, John Steinbeck among them, did go on to work as professional chemists. Courtesy, Monterey County Historical Society

Top: Well into the twentieth century one-room schoolhouses served the educational needs of Salinas Valley children. One such facility was the Blanco School shown here in 1932. Courtesy, Monterey County Library

Above: On August 19, 1920, the cornerstone was laid for the new $400,000 Salinas High School located on Main Street. Courtesy, Monterey County Library

first graduation, with five students receiving their associate of arts degrees. Classes continued to meet at Salinas High School until 1937, when Salinas Junior College moved to its own campus on Homestead Avenue. In 1948 the Board of Trustees changed the name to Hartnell College, reestablishing the ties between the first "college" and the present one.

The 1940s saw major changes for Hartnell College in addition to its new name. In 1947 an agricultural program was started and the school farm was purchased. Known as Hartnell A & M (Agriculture and Mechanics) or East Campus, the new facility on Alisal Road east of Salinas included 10 buildings and 120 acres of land acquired through the War Surplus Agency. After a fire gutted most of the buildings at East Campus in November 1966, classroom activities were transferred permanently to new facilities on the main campus. The agriculture program was discontinued in 1987 and East Campus was leased out for farming, but Vocational Arts classes continue to be one of the focuses of the college.

The decade of the 1940s also saw a rapid increase in enrollment; Hartnell College became the largest junior college between San Francisco and Los Angeles. And in 1948 the Hartnell Junior College District was created, granting representation on the Board of Trustees to all parts of the Valley.

Early on, culture was evident beyond the walls of the Valley's schools. As the largest city, Salinas had a majority of the facilities and opportunities to attract major performances and notables. Besides the excitement and entertainment generated by the annual Rodeo and its "Big Week," Salinas also had at least one opera house, and for a while two, with famous celebrities like John Philip Sousa gracing the stage in addition to some fine local talent. The Chautauqua Program, a traveling cultural event, visited Salinas in 1916 and again in 1919. In August 1925 the Egyptian Tent Theatre was set up at Alisal and Monterey streets opposite Hayward Lumber Company and

an invitation was sent out to "Honest Sinners and Saintly Hypocrites."

By 1946 a Monterey County Symphony was founded to serve the Valley as well as the Monterey Peninsula.

Much as these cultural organizations and events ministered to the spirit of the Valley's residents, medical practitioners and facilities ministered to their bodies. One of the earliest was Dr. S.M. Archer, who established his practice north of Salinas at Santa Rita and built a hospital there in 1865. Though private, it soon came to be used as a county hospital.

The facility had 30 rooms, 24 sleeping apartments, a 12-bed ward, and a dining room. Verandas ran around the buildings allowing patients a fresh-air alternative to their rooms. A building of 10 rooms was set aside for women patients.

At the turn of the century, Salinas doctors S.B. Gordon, T.C. Edwards, and Garth Parker

Above: William E.P. Hartnell, photographed in 1840 at age 39, established "El Colegio de San Jose" at Salinas. The adobe buildings that Hartnell had used for his "Colegio" stood until 1960, when they were razed to discourage the sightseers who plagued the landowner. Courtesy, Hartnell College Library Archives

Above: This Spanish-style building served as Hartnell College's administration and classroom facility from its construction in 1937 until it was razed in 1978 to make room for a new three-story complex. Courtesy, Hartnell College Library Archives

Top: By 1980 the Hartnell College enrollment reached 10,000 students, and major construction had occurred on the Homestead Avenue campus. Seen here at right is the Classroom/Administration building. The College Center is on the left. Courtesy, Jerome Kasavan Associates

Above: As this illustration from Elliott's History of Monterey County *shows, Dr. S.M. Archer's hospital at Santa Rita met the Valley's medical needs in a rural setting. Although it was a private infirmary, it served for many years as the county hospital. Courtesy, Denzil and Jennie Verardo*

opened that city's first hospital in a portion of the old Globe Hotel. In 1906 the Jim Bardin Hospital, a Main Street landmark for many years, opened. Although supported by Bardin, the hospital proved to be a "losing proposition from the start" and was closed in 1912. Several other health care facilities followed; the modern Salinas Valley Memorial Hospital, the Valley's main private care provider, opened in April 1953.

In South County, Dr. L.M. Andrus had established King City's first hospital in 1932. In 1962 Mee Memorial Hospital moved into its present modern facilities, having originally been organized in 1958 with a donation from George and Myrtle Mee of Peachtree.

Virtually dozens of churches, temples, and synagogues have served the spiritual needs of the Valley, beginning with the founding of the missions in the eighteenth century. The Catholic faith was soon joined by Protestant faiths as American settlers brought their religious traditions along with them to the West. By 1881 seven churches stood in the city of Salinas, including Episcopal, Methodist Episcopal, Methodist Episcopal Church South, Presbyterian, Baptist, and United Presbyterian, in addition to Sacred Heart Catholic Church, the oldest permanent church in the

town. Most of these churches had been established in Salinas in the 1870s and 1880s.

Neighboring communities in the Valley seem to have had a similar pattern: "Within seven years of its founding [1886], King City boasted three fine new churches . . . " according to the *History of Monterey County*. In Castroville in the 1880s, "the churches were two in number, the larger one being the Catholic . . . The Union Church building is used by all Protestant denominations." Soledad had, in addition to its Catholic mission, a Union church in the late 1800s.

The Salinas Valley also felt the impact, spiritually and physically, of another religious group, the Salvation Army. In 1897 Commander Booth purchased almost 600 acres near Mission Soledad from Charles T. Romie, county supervisor and brother-in-law of wealthy landowner David Jacks. Nineteen years earlier, Romie had attempted unsuccessfully to sell his Mission Ranch in 10-acre parcels for $20 an acre. Now the poor and homeless from San Francisco's slums were given a chance to make a new life for themselves in the former mission fields.

One of three such colonies established in the United States, the Fort Romie colony originally consisted of 19 families who were each

Above: Our Lady of Refuge Catholic Church, whose altar is shown here at the turn of the century, was originally the mother parish for Salinas City, Gonzales, Soledad, and King City. Although the Catholic faith was the first non-native religion to arrive in the Valley, it was soon joined by a wide variety of others. Courtesy, Denzil and Jennie Verardo

Top: The Salinas Valley Sanitarium, located on the southeast corner of Pajaro and San Luis streets, was one of Salinas' early hospitals. Shown standing in front of the building are Dr. T.C. Edwards, left, and Dr. John Parker, right, with four of the sanitarium's nurses. Courtesy, Monterey County Historical Society

Located about four miles southwest of Soledad, the Salvation Army's Fort Romie Colony was an attempt to give poor and homeless families a second chance at life by providing them land to farm in the Salinas Valley. Photo by Lewis Slevin. Courtesy, Monterey County Library

given 10-acre tracts with an army-built two-room house, on the condition that they work the land and, from the sale of their farm products, repay the Salvation Army about $80 per acre, in installments. Seeds, tools, and equipment were provided, as were encouragement and moral teachings. A townsite was laid out on communal property and it included public buildings, creameries, and a cooperative store. Most of the Fort Romie colonists raised hay or had dairy or truck crop farms. For a while, it appeared that the experiment would provide an effective way of dealing with the poor from the city. The initial success of the communal venture became so famous, in fact, that poet Rudyard Kipling visited it from England. Eventually though, many of the colonists, lured by great profits, sold their land to local farmers for many times what they had paid to the Salvation Army, and the Fort Romie Colony became a memory.

On the other side of the Valley at the foot of the Gabilans opposite Spence Switch, St. Joseph's Colony developed in 1897. For an investment of $1,200, German Catholic families were given the opportunity to settle here. The German Colonization Association of California, Inc., headed by President August Erz and local supporters F.H. Lang and Judge N.A. Dorn, advertised that theirs was "no pauper scheme, and every detail of our colony has been examined carefully by a committee composed of representatives from several states." They went on to say in an 1897 *Salinas Index* article that what they sought were "men who will go to work on the farms of the state and develop its resources."

Almost daily, trains brought families to the new community from Germany by way of Chicago. A store, a post office, a two-story hotel, a saloon, and a church that also served as the school anchored the colony.

Unfortunately for the 100 or so settlers, the soil in the area made farming unprofitable for the former tradesmen. Poor soil coupled with a drought during the colony's early years forced many to abandon St. Joseph's. Lang bought back some of the property, and by 1907 the last of the colonists had admitted defeat. The former St. Joseph's Colony now belonged to the Bardin family. The church was moved in two parts to Spreckels, where it served for many years as the St. Joseph's Parish Catholic Church.

Below: Organized in December 1874 as the Excelsior Hose Company and the Alert Hook and Ladder Company, the Salinas Fire Department was located on West Gabilan Street, adjacent to the Togo Shoe Store and the Salinas Index Printing Office when this photo was taken circa 1910. Courtesy, Monterey County Library

Above: By 1930 most of the Fort Romie Colony had been abandoned. Its shuttered school, photographed in 1930, serves as a reminder of the noble effort to improve conditions for the urban poor in the late 1800s. Photo by Lewis Slevin. Courtesy, Monterey County Historical Society

CHAPTER FIVE

Eureka! Green Gold!

———

The most fertile lands in California lie . . .
along the margin of the Salinas . . .
[T]hese and other insular spots, may be
made perfect gardens.
—Walter Colton, 1845

The Salinas Valley grows 45 to 50 percent
of the nation's total commercial lettuce
crop . . . nowhere else in the United States
does so small an agricultural area produce
so large a percentage of a widely
consumed commercial crop.
—Scientific Monthly, *1955*

The annual California Rodeo in Salinas provided a valuable morale boost during the Depression years. The parades, entertainment, and events associated with the rodeo allowed families a break from the tedious economic news. In 1939 Levi Strauss provided entertainment at the rodeo to "show off their Levis." Courtesy, Monterey County Historical Society

Walter Colton's nineteenth-century prophecy came to fruition in the second decade of the twentieth century, although until after World War I no one could have predicted that the Salinas Valley would be transformed into the nation's salad bowl.

With the outbreak of war in August 1914, previously unknown European place-names such as Verdun and Somme became headline news throughout the Salinas Valley. While the United States had not yet entered the war, the confrontation was a concern, heightened by the fact that the Valley had a relatively large European immigrant population (between 15 and 20 percent of the total population), mostly from Italy, Switzerland, and Germany. Governor Hiram Johnson's visit to the area in October 1914 and speech before 500 area residents at the King City Opera House was a welcome break from the daily news of the war.

During the war, demand for the Salinas Valley's agricultural and dairy products was high. At first, as the United States clung to neutrality, agricultural products such as dry beans became a lucrative crop as both the Allied and Central powers needed foodstuffs for the war effort. With America's entry into the war in 1917, prices went even higher as wartime food supplies were rapidly depleted.

Sugar was rationed for the first time during World War I. Germany and France were unable to harvest their beet crop due to the war, and both met their demand by trading with other countries. The world price for sugar soared as demand far exceeded supply. Spreckels' refinery expanded as sugar prices rose and the government urged increased domestic production to alleviate the wartime shortage.

Aside from the positive stimulus provided to

agriculture by the wartime economy, the "War to End All Wars" took on a much more personal note when the United States entered the conflict. Ten million registered for war service in 1917, of which 687,000 were needed in the first call for the national army. A random lottery was conducted to choose those to be drafted. Quotas were established for each local draft board, which had the responsibility of inducting those registered according to their position in the lottery. Monterey County's quota was 1,700 men, the majority of whom were from the Salinas Valley. The entire Valley waited tensely. On July 20, 1917, the first serial numbers were selected in the "great national lottery," held in a committee room of the Senate Office Building in Washington, D.C.

In addition to those newly inducted, Troop C of the National Guard from Salinas was mobilized on August 4, 1917. The harsh reality of war struck home as Troop C marched with family and friends toward the Southern Pacific Railroad Depot in Salinas while the local band played "Stars and Stripes Forever."

The federal government had begun the

Facing page: The U.S. participation in World War I was largely financed through the sale of Liberty Bonds to the public. Publicity promoting the bonds was widespread, and newspapers published articles and ads daily pushing for sales. A sales booth to facilitate the purchase of Liberty Bonds was opened in the main business district in Salinas. Courtesy, Monterey County Historical Society

Above: In 1917 the first airplane landed in Salinas at Carr Flats. A large crowd gathered to watch the landing and the take-off, as the Salinas Valley residents were viewing a flying machine for the first time. Courtesy, Pat Hathaway Photographs

sale of Liberty Bonds to aid in financing the war effort. By 1918 Liberty Bond demonstrations took place in virtually every Salinas Valley community. Red Cross auxiliaries marched down the main streets of the area's towns to stimulate the purchase of bonds. A Liberty Bond sales booth was even erected in downtown Salinas. Wartime patriotism was the theme of the 1917, 1918, and 1919 California Rodeo Colmo parades.

By the end of 1918, however, the war be-

Above: The California Rodeo had started out quietly as a side show to local horse racing. By 1918 the rodeo was well established and offered some diversion to a community concerned with the war in Europe. The 1917, 1918, and 1919 rodeos all featured wartime patriotism as their theme. Courtesy, Monterey County Library

Below: The Salinas Valley entered the modern era with the advent of World War I. The 1919 rodeo emphasized both the new era and the area's historic roots as both airplane and stagecoach races were featured at the event. Courtesy, Monterey County Library

gan to take its toll on the spirit of the community. A change in tone occurred in the printed news about the draft lottery, as the local media reflected the weariness of the people. The *Salinas Daily Index* began to print the names of those inducted without fanfare as the war, and its lottery inductions, continued.

Fortunately, the war was soon over. On November 11, 1918, the *Salinas Daily Index* ran a one-word banner headline that took up a quarter of its front page: "PEACE!" Businesses closed for the day and celebrations continued into the evening as the local population anticipated the return of its youthful veterans.

As a new decade approached, the Salinas Valley looked much as it had in the 1870s, with farming conducted most intensively along the margins of the Salinas River. A journey down the Salinas Valley in 1870 or 1920 would have found an abundance of grain, forage, and hay products, with cattle roaming occasionally in nearby fields.

Irrigation had allowed cultivated acreage to expand, but grains were still the Valley's dominant agricultural crop with some 95,000 acres farmed. Barley was the area's leading

grain followed by wheat, oats, and corn. Barley was grown on all the benchland in the Salinas Valley and wheat was predominant south of King City. In 1920 grain was still hauled to market with wagons pulled by horses, and many farmers still utilized horses to cultivate their fields.

Hay and alfalfa production occupied 76,000 acres of the Salinas Valley. Alfalfa, which relied heavily on irrigation and was associated with the dairy industry, was concentrated in the Gonzales and Soledad area. One contemporary stated that "dairy cattle, pasturing knee-deep in green alfalfa are familiar scenes in the Salinas Valley."

But between 1870 and 1920, some signifi-

In 1922 not a single railcar of lettuce was shipped out of the Salinas Valley. By the end of the 1920s, Salinas became the economic center of California for the production of row crops. The value of the Valley's vegetable crop was in excess of $16 million. In the 1930s modern machinery was used wherever possible, but the bulk of the harvest was still labor intensive. Courtesy, Pat Hathaway Photographs

cant changes had occurred in the Valley's agricultural patterns. Sugar beets had been planted on over 23,000 acres and dry beans and peas occupied another 18,000. Sugar beets were cultivated in King City area fields, and large concentrations were cultivated near Castroville. The first major use of labor contractors in the Salinas Valley was by sugar-beet growers during this period. To thin and harvest their crops, these farmers needed a large labor force for a seasonal period of time. Labor contractors hired out their crews by the job, relieving the farmer of time-consuming hiring and supervisory responsibility. By contracting for labor, costs could also be kept below the prevailing 1920 wage of 41 cents an hour. The Salinas Valley's primary contract laborers in 1920 were Japanese, Chinese, Mexican, and Filipino workers.

The World War I demand for dry beans, which made them a lucrative crop in the King City and Greenfield area, faded with the war. In 1919 the price of this crop plummeted and acreage was reduced. The remaining acreage cultivated in the Salinas Valley in 1920 was made up of fruit orchards, which occupied 5,000 acres, and potatoes, which were planted on 2,000 acres along the Salinas River between Spreckels and the river's mouth. All other vegetables combined occupied only a little over 550 acres of land, with lettuce planted on a total of 60 acres.

In 1920 farmland in the Salinas Valley could still be purchased for $50 an acre, although the more desirable irrigated parcels could bring $300. The largest landholder in the Salinas Valley was the Spreckels Sugar Company, which controlled virtually all the land along the Salinas River to Soledad, as well as the flood-plain around King City. Large ranches still occupied a good deal of the Valley with the following approximate holdings: the Jacks Company (24,000 acres); Mrs. J.B. Espinosa (11,000 acres); the Brandenstein Co. (8,700 acres); J.A. Trescony (8,400 acres); the Salinas Land Co. (8,400 acres); the Arroyo Seco Todos Santos Land and Invest-

ment Company (7,300 acres); Anita Purdy (6,400 acres); Teresa Johnson (5,700 acres); C.D. Field (5,700 acres); and Thomas Doud (5,700 acres).

In 1920 nearly 220,000 acres were under cultivation, a figure which would not increase in a significant way until the 1940s. What *was* significant was the incredible transformation that occurred between these two decades. The Salinas Valley of 1920, with its 60 acres of lettuce and 95,000 of grain, would not be recognizable by 1940.

The population of Monterey County in 1920 numbered 28,000; 15,000 people lived in the Salinas Valley, 4,000 in the city of Salinas. The Valley's growth had hardly been dramatic up to this time. The county's population in 1880 had been 11,302, 1,865 in the city of Salinas. Between 1880 and 1920 Salinas' population only a little more than doubled. Between 1900 and 1910 California's population grew 45 percent and between 1910 and 1920 it grew 60 percent. Salinas only grew 19 and 13 percent during these same decades. But in the 1920s the population of the Salinas Valley would increase by an explosive 95 percent, illustrating the dynamic change that occurred beginning in this period. The Salinas Valley was poised to enter one of the most significant decades in its agricultural, economic, and demographic history.

This change was signaled at the end of 1919 when the Spreckels Sugar Company's beet acreage peaked. Decreased demand brought about by the end of World War I caused sugar prices to fall. It became economically unfeasible to harvest the quantities of beets that had been harvested in the past. Acreage planted in beets was withdrawn and planted in more economical crops such as beans and barley.

During this same period, blight and nematode infestations occurred on all Spreckels' ranches except those in the northern portion of the Salinas Valley. Crops had not been rotated on the southern ranches and the resulting soil depletion allowed curly top disease to strike the beet plants. Seed quality was also declining. The

In the Salinas Valley the Depression created not only a shortage of jobs and poor wages, but also a critical shortage of affordable housing. Shantytowns sprung up in many communities. The Gonzales Passenger Coach Colony, shown in this photo, at least provided a roof over residents' heads. Photo by Lewis Slevin. Courtesy, Monterey County Historical Society

northern ranches were planted on the rich Salinas River deposits and were the most valuable of all Spreckels' properties. Unfortunately for the sugar company, these ranches were farmed under lease agreements with the owners. With the plummeting prices, Spreckels could not afford to offer high rentals for extended leases. As a result, the sugar company lost its best beet acreage to other crops.

The 23,000 acres of beets in 1920 declined to 13,000 by 1925 and to only 200 acres by 1929. At the same time beet prices dropped to the point where an acre of sugar beets might yield only a $50 return. Sugar beet growing in the Salinas Valley was essentially eliminated, although the Spreckels Sugar Company refinery continued to play an important economic role. Because it no longer raised significant amounts of its own beets, the Spreckels Company acquired its supply from sources where it could control the price of purchase.

The decline in sugar prices and the withdrawal of beet acreage occurred at the same time that row crop vegetables were being introduced. Crops such as lettuce, artichokes, and broccoli may have eventually displaced sugar beets anyway, but the rapid and dramatic transformation of the Salinas Valley must in part be attributed to the availability of thousands of acres of prime agricultural land, land that the Spreckels Sugar Company could not keep in production.

Rancho Bolsa del Potrero y Moro Cojo illustrates this rapid change. In 1888 the Moro Cojo ranch near Castroville was leased by the Spreckels Sugar Company from the heirs of the original grantee, J.B.R. Cooper. In 1921 the company's lease on the Moro Cojo was due, but with the declining beet situation, Spreckels could not afford to offer the same rent or terms on the property. Andrew J. Molera, Cooper's grandson, who, with his sister, now owned the property, looked elsewhere for a return on his land. Artichokes were new to the U.S. market, but Molera was convinced they could be raised on his ranch. His family had already grown them as a garden vegetable, and they were grown commercially, on a limited scale, in San Mateo County near Half Moon Bay. Best of all, the artichoke commanded a high market price, and artichoke farmers would be able to pay Molera nearly triple the rent the Spreckels Company was willing to pay for the same land.

Molera agreed to furnish some of the plants for the initial crop and to drill wells to supply the new fields. Molera then began leasing 75 to 150 acres directly to farmers. The first planting of artichokes in Monterey County was made in the spring of 1922, and some 600 acres were in production by the fall of that year. By 1925 over 4,000 acres of artichokes were cultivated. Angelo and Dan Del Chiaro, Dan Pieri, Alfred Tottino, and Jim Bellone, who all had taken advantage of Molera's original lease arrangements, formed the California Artichoke and Vegetable Growers Corporation in 1924 with a loan from A.P. Giannini of San Francisco. In 1904 Giannini had begun his own business, the Bank of Italy, precursor of today's Bank of America. The California Artichoke and Vegetable Growers would soon dominate the national artichoke market through their effective growing and distribution systems. By 1929 artichokes were the Salinas Valley's third largest cash crop.

In 1932 an artichoke standardization law was passed by the state legislature in an effort to regulate the quality of the vegetable. Unfortunately, growers began to take losses from the prohibition they had imposed on the shipment of artichokes with frostbitten stems, even though the quality of the artichokes was unaffected. In 1937 a cold snap caused over $10,000 worth of artichokes to be lost because the standardization

law prohibited shipment. Growers rose in protest to overturn the law. Fifty-five growers, representing 80 percent of the acreage planted in artichokes, requested that the state's agricultural committee support their cause. Led by pioneer grower Dan Pieri, support was given to a bill that would change the law. Castroville had become the "Artichoke Capital of the World," politically as well as economically. In recent decades the Castroville area has produced some 80 percent of the world's supply of artichokes.

While artichokes filled an agricultural void in the northern Salinas Valley left by declining sugar beet cultivation, it was lettuce that would lead an agricultural revolution in the rest of the area. After the first successful experimental plantings, lettuce production exploded. In early 1922 approximately 300 acres of lettuce were planted around Salinas. By the end of the year the acreage had doubled to nearly 600. By 1927, 13,500 acres had been planted; by 1928, 35,000; and by the end of the decade, 43,000 acres of the Salinas Valley were planted in lettuce.

In 1922 not a single railcar of lettuce was shipped out of the area—all was produced for local markets. But a major agricultural breakthrough occurred in 1923 with the introduction of the ice-bunkered refrigerated railcar. Within five years some 18,000 railcars of lettuce, requiring over 160,000 tons of ice, left the Salinas Valley for the East Coast. This amounted to 33 percent of the nation's total production, and more than the competing Imperial Valley in California ever shipped in one year. By 1930 more than 20,000 cars per year were being shipped out of the area. A record was broken in May 1928 when Salinas shipped 230 cars in one day.

A list of the top 10 products produced in the Salinas Valley in 1919 showed sugar beets at the top of the list. By 1929 lettuce not only took the place of beets on that top 10 list, but it accounted for nearly $6 million of the $16 million total of those top 10 products, and bank deposits in Salinas ranked it as one of the nation's wealthiest per capita cities. Only 50 years later the Salinas Valley's lettuce value would top $171 million.

The growth of lettuce production in the Salinas Valley in the 1920s was aided by a distinct national trend toward the consumption of head lettuce, the predominant variety grown in the area. Between the beginning of the decade and 1925 the annual per capita consumption of iceberg lettuce increased from one to five heads. The increased demand for lettuce was such that nearly 80 percent of the entire crop produced was absorbed by the eastern markets without dropping in price. The remaining 20 percent went to other parts of the country.

Salinas competed well with Southern California because of its ability to grow lettuce through the summer months, an accomplishment not possible in the warm southland. One of the first individuals to experiment with a summer crop was Frank McFadden. McFadden planted 25 acres of lettuce in June 1923 in the face of much skepticism. However, his planting yielded over 7,000 crates of lettuce, most of which was sold and shipped to Los Angeles—the heart of the competitor's market. McFadden's skeptics vanished as he had made more than $14,000 profit (in 1923 dollars) with his small planting of summer lettuce.

Salinas soon became the economic center of California for the production of lettuce. Buyers, sellers, inspectors, transportation agents, and market agents all settled in the area. By the end of the twenties, nearly 40 major packing sheds had been constructed, as well as ice plants, paper suppliers, and numerous other support industries.

Lettuce is a heavily irrigated crop. In 1928 some 3,000 horsepower of pumping machinery was utilized to water the Valley's lettuce fields, and the Coast Valleys Gas and Electric Company strung an extensive network of power lines through the area, which not only serviced the pumps, but allowed complete rural electrification to occur.

Other truck crops—cauliflower, tomatoes, celery, and carrots, as well as products such as potatoes, peas, and apricots—were all successful during the decade of the 1920s. Salinas was even purported to have the largest strawberry farm in the world.

In the 1920s broccoli seeds were imported from France and Italy by Stephen and Andrew D'Arrigo and introduced to the U.S. market. In 1927 Thomas Chesholm planted 100 acres of broccoli in the Salinas Valley near Spreckels, the largest planting up to that time in the area. He sent his goods to the D'Arrigo Bros. Company in San Jose for sorting, packing, and shipping to East Coast markets. The venture was successful and D'Arrigo Bros. soon expanded their operations. They marketed broccoli in 1928 and 1929 through Italian-language radio programs in Boston and effectively used advertising to expand to other major East Coast cities. D'Arrigo Bros. Company eventually became the largest broccoli producer in the U.S. and the crop became one of the leading agricultural products in the Salinas Valley.

Nothing short of an agricultural revolution had taken place in the area in the 1920s.

The residents of the county seat adopted a new city charter which went into effect in mid-1919 and changed the name of their town from Salinas City to the City of Salinas. The new charter also provided for five council members to be elected at large, with the mayor to be selected from the council. The new City of Salinas also modernized its fire department, eliminating horses from its work force. Under Warren King, Chief of the King City Fire Department from 1916 to 1933, that city also modernized and upgraded its fire services by eliminating horses and ordering new, modern America-LaFrance state-of-the-art pumper units.

In 1919 the City of Salinas made a major change in its revenue sources by shifting its primary funding from liquor licenses to property taxes. This revenue shift occurred none too soon as the 18th Amendment to the Constitution (Prohibition) went into effect in January 1920.

Salinas Valley newspapers reported numerous raids by federal enforcement agents working with local law officers as Prohibition was strictly enforced in the area. One local incident known as the "Moss Landing Rum Battle" made statewide headlines and national news. Moss Landing was often frequented by small boats smuggling illicit liquor for distribution in the area. In April 1925 county law enforcement officers had received a tip that one such smuggling launch point was in the Moss Landing area, and a sheriff's posse was sent to investigate. As the posse passed through an open field in Moss Landing, it was ambushed and fired upon by the machine-gun wielding smugglers.

Special officer N.H. Rader was killed, and Sheriff W.A. Oyer and Traffic Officer Henry J. Livingston were wounded. The local constable was uninjured, but had a cigarette shot from his mouth in the hail of gunfire. Numerous suspects were arrested and two went to trial on murder charges.

Noted Pebble Beach artist Joseph Jacinto Mora sculpted the concrete busts which adorn the Monterey County courthouse. Each represents a significant historical figure who contributed greatly to the area. The courthouse was dedicated on October 30, 1937. Courtesy, Monterey County Historical Society

Politically, the Salinas Valley mirrored the rest of California and the nation during this period. From 1920 to 1930, Monterey County voted Republican in every gubernatorial election, and no Democratic partisan candidate won an election in the county.

With the stock market crash of 1929, and the ensuing Great Depression, the Salinas Valley's 1920s prosperity ended for many individuals. In 1932, when Franklin Delano Roosevelt was elected president of the United States, the Salinas Valley was a recipient of many of the beneficial effects of his national recovery program. The 1933 National Industrial Recovery Act included formation of the Public Works Administration (PWA), which facilitated and financed the completion of major public works projects for the area. The PWA planned the projects and then contracted with local firms for the construction phase, thereby stimulating the stagnant local economy.

Parks, sewers, storm drains, the Salinas Municipal Golf Course, a post office, additions to the county hospital, and highway projects were all part of the PWA's accomplishments during the

Depression. One project, a new $500,000 county courthouse, received approval for matching funds by the area's voters. Noted Pebble Beach artist Joseph Jacinto Mora, originally a native of Uruguay, created 62 concrete sculptured heads to adorn the outer walls of the courthouse. The sculptures represent people important to the county's history, including Indians, women, and trappers, as well as specific individuals such as Cabrillo, Junipero Serra, and John C. Fremont. The county courthouse was dedicated in Salinas on October 30, 1937. Although some deterioration has taken place over the years, Joseph Mora's sculptures still evoke the Salinas Valley's historic past.

Another public works project called for expenditure of funds for the American Legion Airport in North Salinas. Originally completed in 1929 through the efforts of the Salinas American Legion and operated by them, the public airport needed improving. In 1935 the California State Emergency Relief Administration lengthened runways and added an airplane hangar and weather station. The airport was still insufficient for the area's needs, however, and the Works Progress Administration (WPA) in 1940 allocated $310,000 for the construction of runways for a new Salinas Municipal Airport. Once completed, the field became a U.S. Army Air Corps Base. The City of Salinas contributed an additional $25,000 to the project. Salinas City Engineer Donald Davies'

airport master plan was lauded by the WPA as one of "the finest engineering projects ever submitted for approval."

The WPA also developed programs designed to help artists. One segment of the WPA, the Federal Writers Project, published *California: A Guide to the Golden State,* which included a segment on the Salinas Valley. Numerous other national recovery projects, sponsored by one of the myriad of FDR's federal agencies, assisted the Salinas Valley during the Depression years.

With the creation of the Agricultural Adjustment Administration (AAA) in 1933, Salinas Valley farmers also received federal benefits. The economy of the Salinas Valley largely was kept intact during the Depression because of the stability and increasing productivity of its agricultural commodities. California's financial institutions had a major vested interest in promoting the successful

The Public Works Administration, one of President Franklin Delano Roosevelt's recovery agencies during the Great Depression, provided matching funds for the construction of a new county courthouse in Salinas. Shown here under construction, the courthouse was completed at a cost of $500,000. Courtesy, Monterey County Historical Society

In 1937 an FBI training program was held in Salinas for law enforcement officials. It was the first professional training program on crime prevention and detection ever given in the area. The first graduates of the school are seen here. Courtesy, Monterey County Historical Society

sales of the Valley's crops. In 1930 A.P. Giannini's Bank of Italy alone had 1,456 outstanding loans on farms in the Santa Clara and Salinas valleys totaling $14,520,691! A collapse in farm commodities would spell disaster for banking institutions.

Thus the AAA's programs, and its support payments to farmers, were lauded by a wide range of institutions who had an economic interest in Salinas Valley agriculture.

Through the AAA, farmers could receive subsidy payments under an Agricultural Conservation Program if they met several criteria. Applying fertilizer, planting cover crops, eradicating weeds, or constructing dams, to name a few, all qualified a Salinas Valley farmer for support payments. Between 1939 and 1941 farmers received over $350,000 in payments for soil maintenance and conservation which would not have been done without the Agricultural Conservation Program subsidies—a small price to pay for a region that produced more than $17 million in agricultural commodities per year. During this period the Salinas Valley was considered by the Farm Bureau as the "bright spot in the state, if not the nation . . . the one place . . . where farmers

made fortunes tilling the soil."

Another AAA government subsidy to local farmers was made under the Sugar Act. As previously mentioned, sugar beet acreage had declined to negligible amounts by the end of the 1920s as farmers turned to more profitable crops. However, in 1930 a duty was placed on sugar entering the U.S. This tariff protected the domestic sugar market from the worldwide glut that lowered prices to the point of making it uneconomical. Sugar beets were again planted in the Salinas Valley for processing at the local Spreckels plant. Unfortunately, the Depression offset the protection a tariff normally would have afforded, and sugar prices still declined. As farmers increased production to maintain their revenues, prices dropped even more. By the mid-1930s over 10,000 acres of the Salinas Valley were again planted in beets.

To receive payments under the Sugar Act, farmers had to plant no more land to beets than would be approved by the AAA, and had to apply fertilizers to maintain their soils. Payments to local farmers between 1939 and 1941 totaled more than $2 million, making it profitable to plant despite declining prices. Unfortunately, the subsidies did increase the production of sugar beets beyond that which could be readily marketed. In 1938 some 20,000 acres in the Valley were once again devoted to the growing of sugar beets.

Under the Sugar Act the federal government

also required that fair and reasonable wages be paid to sugar beet laborers. This wage policy had perhaps the greatest impact on the Salinas Valley as a result of the Depression—an influx of new agricultural workers to the area from more severely depressed countries, as well as from other economically depressed areas of the United States. The resultant changes brought about during this period altered the working relationship between farmer and laborer.

Farm owners throughout California had long used the least expensive labor possible to harvest their crops, and the Salinas Valley was no exception. At the same time, the people who cultivated crops had to be industrious and hardy to cope with the backbreaking requirements of an agricultural harvest. Historically, the situation had begun with Franciscan missionaries using Indian labor to tend their crops.

In the 1860s Chinese were imported to work on Western railroad construction, but the completion of the transcontinental railroad in 1869 made available thousands of these workers. Growers were quick to hire this cheap source of labor. By 1880, 90 percent of all field work was done by Chinese workers. With the passage of the Chinese Exclusion Act in 1882, farmers turned to Japan to supply their needs. By 1913 over 75,000 Japanese were working in fields in the West. When Japanese workers began to buy land of their own, the California legislature passed the Alien Land Act of 1913, under which land owned by Japanese aliens could be confiscated by the state.

During World War I thousands of field workers entered California from Mexico, supplementing the predominant Japanese laborers. The Immigration Act of 1924 essentially excluded further Japanese entry into the United States. After restrictions were imposed on Chinese and Japanese immigration, Filipino workers filled the void. By 1920 Filipinos were employed in relatively large numbers in the Salinas Valley, and by 1940 the Filipino population in the Salinas Valley was one of the largest in California.

By the end of the 1920s, in large part because of the automobile, workers harvesting seasonal crops could migrate from one area to another, following harvests. The Depression struck with this labor situation in place. Then one of the greatest internal migrations in U.S. history occurred. Only the Gold Rush rivals the trek to California which took place in the 1930s. In that decade, dust storms swept across the plains of states such as Oklahoma, Arkansas, and Texas, making farming a virtual impossibility. An enormous influx of uprooted tenant farmers came to California's agricultural communities seeking employment, and the productive Salinas Valley was a primary destination. The plight of these Depression-relocated Americans was immortalized by John Steinbeck in his *Grapes of Wrath*. By 1934 more than 50 percent of the population in agricultural labor camps were uprooted Americans looking for a better way of life, much as earlier immigrants from other countries had done. But these "huddled masses" were Americans.

In the 1930s Elton Hebbron, a grower who owned 120 acres east of Salinas, subdivided his land into small lots and sold them to the new migrants. Soon East Salinas' "Little Oklahoma" was the largest concentration of new immigrants in the Salinas Valley and one of the largest in the state. By 1935 more than 4,000 agricultural workers from Oklahoma, Arkansas, and Texas had settled in the area.

Labor was one cost over which farmers could exert control. Wages were depressed, and growers were reluctant to raise them even when prices improved since they faced other uncontrollable fixed costs. Field labor had been paid 40 cents per hour in the 1920s, but that rate fell to a low of 15 cents an hour in the early years of the Depression. Public labor camps were subsidized by the government in an effort to alleviate the plight of the agricultural workers. All the elements were in place for potential conflict between growers and agricultural laborers.

CHAPTER SIX

Dubious Battles

And we've got an enemy, see?
Guys work together nice when they've got
an enemy.

—*John Steinbeck,* In Dubious Battle, *1936*

Four of the Salinas Valley's pioneer growers, seen here from the left, are: K.R. Nutting, T.R. Merrill, Bruce Church, and E.E. Harden. The photograph was taken following the bitter agricultural strike at the new Growers Ice and Development plant in Salinas, one of the largest packing shed operations in the nation. Courtesy, Salinas Steinbeck Library

In 1930, in order to control agricultural costs and pool marketing activities, a voluntary trade association was formed, the Grower-Shipper Vegetable Association of Central California. At one time the association represented nearly 75 percent of all growers and shippers in the Salinas Valley and Watsonville areas.

In September 1936 one of the worst agricultural strikes in California history took place in the Salinas Valley. For a short time growers and shippers were crippled by the bitter strike. However, the strike was eventually broken because shed workers were unable to halt the truck and rail shipments guarded and escorted by armed law enforcement officers. Here, lettuce bound for eastern markets is loaded during the strike. Courtesy, Pat Hathaway Photographs

During this same period the Vegetable Packers Union had formed and was gaining strength in the Salinas Valley. The Vegetable Packers Union was affiliated with the American Federation of Labor (AF of L). The AF of L, and the union movement in general, was making rapid inroads across the nation in an effort to unionize America's labor force. The Packers Union was made up mostly of white Anglo workers employed in the packing sheds. Filipino, Mexican, and other ethnic minority agricultural laborers were relegated to field work and, while sympathetic with the Packers Union, were restricted from membership.

Agricultural strikes occurred beginning in 1930 in many parts of California, as workers protested low wages and repressive working condi-

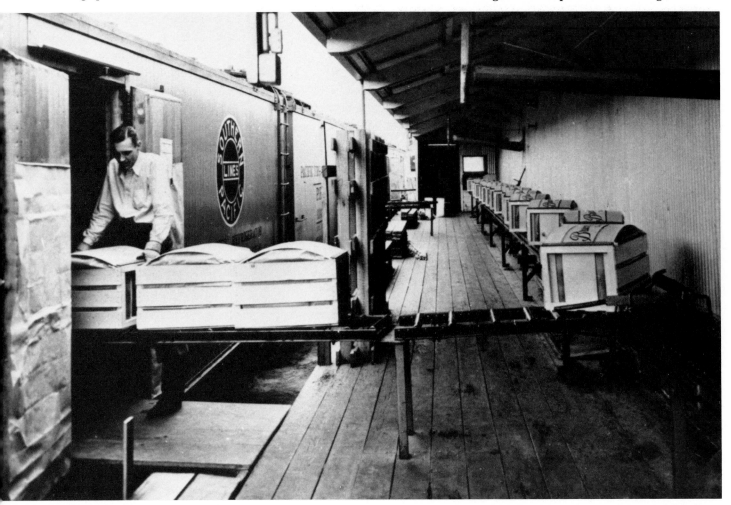

tions. In 1933 an ethnic affiliation of Filipino field workers, the Filipino Labor Union, organized. In August of that year they called a strike against Salinas Valley lettuce growers, protesting low wages and calling for official recognition of their union. The strike was broken, however, when Mexican and Asian laborers were brought in to replace the striking Filipino workers. One year later, in August 1934, the Vegetable Packers Union went on strike, and the Filipino Labor Union working the Valley's lettuce fields joined them. This united front of Filipino field and white shed workers posed a serious threat to the Salinas Valley's growers and shippers. The summer harvest began in August, and growers were faced with the potential loss of their crop. The strike had turbulent moments, especially for Filipino workers, who faced racist animosity. One camp was riddled with bullets and set afire as "vigilantes" attempted to break the strike. The Grower-Shipper Association, however, agreed to demands for arbitration and the strike was settled with an agreement favorable to the Packers Union and the FLU. This was the first serious settlement in California between agricultural growers and organized ethnic workers. Salinas' first agricultural strike had ended.

In August 1936 negotiations again began between growers and the union, now called the Fruit and Vegetable Workers, as the agreement reached in 1934 ended. On September 3 the Grower-Shipper Vegetable Association offered the shed workers a five-cent-per-hour raise in wages with equal pay for men and women. The union demanded preferential hiring, but the growers refused to consider any movement toward the establishment of a "closed shop," although they were willing to recognize the union as an agent representing packing shed employees for collective bargaining purposes. The union rejected the growers' offer and members voted overwhelmingly to strike.

On September 4, the first day of the strike, the *Salinas Index-Journal* reported that the lettuce

"Industry Is Brought to a Standstill." An estimated $12-million lettuce crop sat in the fields. As picketers lined up, the Grower-Shipper Association met in the Cominos Hotel in Salinas to plan their future strategy.

By September 8 the shed workers had been joined in the strike by lettuce truck drivers. It was estimated that growers were losing $75,000 a day. No violence had yet occurred, although verbal exchanges were heated. The union accused the growers of a "lockout" prohibiting workers from entering the packing sheds. The growers countered, arguing that there was no lockout— workers could work at the rates posted in the sheds. Meanwhile, fences were constructed around packing sheds to protect them from the strikers' activities, as well as to prepare them to reopen, in defiance of the shutdown. By now over 3,000 shed workers were on strike, and some 500 Filipino field workers had joined them.

On September 15 the Grower-Shipper Vegetable Association reopened the sheds and began to move lettuce from the fields. More than 2,000 pickets surrounded the Salinas Valley Ice Company, where the first lettuce trucks were to arrive. As the trucks pulled into view, a barrage of rocks shattered windshields, injuring several individuals. The rock throwing was met with tear gas, driving strikers for cover. The violence had begun.

By the following day rioting broke out throughout Salinas, spreading to the main business district. According to the *Index-Journal,* sheriff's deputies and strikers were in "a pitched battle," which resulted in two men shot and several injured. Lettuce trucks were dumped of their loads as strikers blockaded intersections to keep traffic at a standstill.

U.S. Deputy Labor Commissioner Walter Matheson telephoned Timothy Reardon, chairman of the State Industrial Relations Board, to inform him that he would be arriving from Washington, D.C., to investigate the strike. Matheson stated that the strike came under federal jurisdiction since lettuce shipping was interstate commerce. Meanwhile, amid shouts of "we want law and order in Salinas," 600 delegates to the California Federation of Labor Convention in Sacramento paraded around the capital as they waited to see Governor Frank Merriam. The Salinas lettuce strike was now national news.

The Growers Association hired Colonel Henry Sanborn, an army reserve officer and publisher of the conservative *American Citizen,* to take command of their operation against the strikers. While he held no official law enforcement position, he did organize raids and direct arrests of strikers. Sanborn ordered large supplies of tear gas for his operation; an estimated 200 rounds were actually used.

By now Salinas resembled a military zone. Mobs were common. The labor council officers had been bombed with tear gas. A *San Francisco Chronicle* photographer was ordered by growers to "get the hell out of Salinas" or face a lynch mob. Local jails were at capacity and schools and businesses were closed. Airplanes were even sent up to reconnoiter, and 200 troops camped at the rodeo grounds.

Sheriff Carl Abbott called for all "able-bodied men" to report for duty and be sworn in as special deputies to assist with the strike. More than 1,000 individuals responded. This "Citizen's Army" was armed with whatever weapons its members had on hand, and all those not possessing their own arms were issued axe handles that had been made at Salinas High School, despite the protests of some parents.

On September 17, 40 truckloads of lettuce were hauled from the fields to the Salinas Valley Ice Company under the protection of 20 highway patrol cars and numerous autos loaded with armed deputies. The ice company had guards with machine guns on its roof. As the convoy approached, "the green gold parade passed without incident," the *Index-Journal* reported. Union pickets had been called off in the face of insurmountable

odds. Suppliers and the Southern Pacific Railroad as well as the local business community supported the growers and shippers and presented a united front against the union.

The strike was about to be broken.

On September 18, 1936, a law enforcement meeting was held in the Salinas Armory. The keynote speech began, "there is a virtual state of war in this community." One speaker, Colonel Henry Sanborn, implied that Communists were assisting with the strike. But this inflammatory accusation did not fare well with the law enforcement, business, or agricultural communities. The issue was sensitive because an earlier California-based union, the Cannery and Agricultural Workers' Industrial Union (CAWIU), was backed by the Communist party in an effort to organize farm workers. The CAWIU was linked to the strikes of the early 1930s. These early strikes had been bitterly denounced and the leadership of the CAWIU arrested under the Criminal Syndicalism Act. In 1934 all CAWIU leaders were brought to trial and convicted under the act. Thus cries of Communist takeover of the Salinas strike in 1936 had no basis in fact. Henry Sanborn was summarily dismissed and "won't be back," stated Sheriff Abbott.

Governor Merriam tried to intercede in the dispute but was unsuccessful. Meanwhile, although picketing had resumed, lettuce shipments regained lost momentum, reaching almost normal production levels by September 21. A proposal by U.S. Commissioner Matheson and State Labor Secretary Edward Vandeleur was rejected by the union and members stayed off the job. The *Salinas Index-Journal* called for arbitration, stating that the dispute "MUST be settled over the conference table. Only in this way can the rights of both sides be sanely and impassionately weighed and balanced." But their editorial fell on deaf ears.

The WPA then announced that 75 strikers would be put to work on WPA jobs, and stated that if they refused to work, they would be dropped from state relief rolls. Then, on October 2, the union received its biggest blow, making any future success impossible. The Monterey County Board of Supervisors passed an "emergency" antipicketing ordinance over the protests of the Fruit and Vegetable Workers Union. Former Superior Court Judge J.A. Bardin presented the ordinance on behalf of the "agricultural interests of Monterey County."

On November 3, 1936, the strike ended. Union members had voted to terminate their walkout and return to work. Employers said that union men would be taken back as soon as possible, but few of the "scabs" were replaced. Hearings by the National Labor Relations Board revealed that the grower-shippers had planned well in advance for a strike, hiring publicity agents during the strike in an attempt to gain press and community support.

The 1936 Salinas lettuce strike was the most severe ever to hit the Salinas Valley and was one of the worst agricultural strikes in California history. The primary long-term effects of the strike were that growers and shippers maintained control over agricultural wages, at least until the advent of World War II, and postponed union organization of field workers for several decades to come.

Labor in general did make gains during this period, however. In 1937, for example, the AF of L organized the Spreckels Sugar Company refinery workers. Wages were increased, the workweek dropped from seven to six days, and the workday reduced from 12 to 10 hours.

The Depression dealt a severe blow in human terms, but the Salinas Valley suffered less than most of the nation due to the expanding economy provided by the area's agriculture. The development of the lettuce industry alone provided an increased wealth unheard of during this period of U.S. history. At the end of the decade, by 1939, over 1,000 railcars of artichokes, 24,000 cars of lettuce, and 7,000 cars of other vegetables were shipped from the Salinas Valley. Not only was this an all-time high to date, but it represented the greatest production of row crops in the country. The value of the area's agricultural commodities was well over $50 million, an impressive figure for any era, let alone during the worst economic downturn in the nation's history.

In 1920 the population of Salinas was approximately 4,000; in 1940 it was 11,000. The population of the county during the same period grew from some 28,000 to 73,000 people. Most of this population growth is directly attributable to the area's booming economy, relative abundance of jobs, and the fulfilled promise of a comparatively better way of life.

The advent of World War II set in motion a flurry of activity as the country mobilized. With the Japanese attack on Pearl Harbor, California became a preferred location for the establishment of military bases. The Army had access to large land holdings in the state, and the Army Air Corps needed locations that would facilitate defense of the coastline. One of the nation's largest training centers was located at Monterey County's Fort Ord. Sub-posts to Fort Ord became active in the southern part of the Salinas Valley at the Hunter Liggett Military Reservation and at Camp Roberts. The 150,000-acre Hunter Liggett Reservation was, until 1940, part of William Randolph Hearst's ranch, but was given up for military use. Construction boomed at these locations as barracks for personnel were erected and numerous facilities were built for the war effort.

The U.S. Army Air Corps had already begun building its facility at the Salinas Municipal Airport, but the field now saw major service as a base for observation squadrons in the Pacific. The airfield had the advantage of good weather conditions that seldom curtailed flying. Even the Rodeo Grounds in Salinas were used by the Army as a branch garrison of Fort Ord. During the war years the annual rodeo was canceled. But the rodeo grounds would become infamous for its other wartime use as a temporary relocation camp for American citizens of Japanese ancestry.

Immediately after Pearl Harbor, the Federal Bureau of Investigation was given the task of rounding up enemy aliens suspected of subversive activities. Travel was restricted, and the Treasury Department froze assets of many of those individuals. General John L. DeWitt, head of the Western Defense Command, urged that West Coast zones be barred to enemy aliens. Soon, that coastal prohibition went into effect for all enemy aliens, as the War Relocation Authority, a new civilian agency working with the U.S. Army, took over the task of alien evacuation.

In addition to the prohibited coastal area, a restricted zone ran the length of the state. Enemy aliens of Italian, Japanese, and German extraction were prohibited from entering restricted areas without a permit, and strict curfews were enforced. Any violation could result in arrest and internment. In Castroville a white line was painted down the town's main thoroughfare, Merritt Street, to mark the restricted boundary. The west side of the line could not be crossed without a permit. Many people lost their jobs and property due to the restrictions, and hardship cases abounded.

With the outbreak of World War II, the nation's military mobilized rapidly. Fort Ord, shown here in 1940 as troops march past a reviewing stand, was one of the country's largest training centers. The Hunter Liggett Military Reservation and Camp Roberts, which were sub-posts to Fort Ord, were established in the Salinas Valley watershed. Courtesy, Pat Hathaway Photographs

The greatest hardships, however, involved American citizens of Japanese ancestry who were included in the relocation. On March 23, 1942, the first Japanese-American citizens were "evacuated" to Manzanar in the Owens Valley of California for internment during the war.

The California Rodeo Grounds in Salinas was one of several locations utilized as an assembly center for those of Japanese extraction en route to internment camps. Over 180 barracks were constructed on the rodeo grounds, holding over 3,500 individuals at its full capacity. Each evacuee received a number as they registered at the center and was assigned a barrack, and, as if further humiliation were necessary, even had to supply their own bedding. Military guards were on duty 24 hours a day at the facility.

Perhaps the greatest human impact of World War II on the Salinas Valley, however, was on the families of those who went to fight and never returned. Company C of the 194th Battalion from Salinas was sent to Corregidor and Bataan in the Philippines. This company was in the infamous "Bataan Death March" and sustained some of the war's heaviest losses. Only 46 men from Company C survived the ordeal.

The flurry of economic activity to supply the war effort actually ended the Great Depression. Both industry and agriculture in the Salinas Valley contributed in a major way to the war economy.

Magnesium became a critically important war material during the conflict. One of California's most important deposits of dolomite, a mineral from which magnesium can be obtained, lay near Salinas at Natividad. Small amounts of dolomite had been extracted between 1900 and 1925, but not until the Pacific Coast Steel Company began quarrying operations in 1926 was large-scale removal undertaken. In 1937 the Pacific Coast Steel Company was succeeded by the Bethlehem Steel Company, which quarried dolomite at the Natividad site until 1944.

In 1942 the Permanente Metals Corporation, which became the Kaiser Aluminum and Chemical Corporation, also began a dolomite quarry at Natividad, and opened a processing plant in the same area. A seawater magnesia plant was constructed at Moss Landing to supply the raw materials necessary for magnesium metal production. The Salinas Valley dolomite mining operation was the largest in the United States during this period and was part of the biggest carbothermic magnesium-making operation in the world. After the war a refractory brick plant was also built at Moss Landing to utilize the excess magnesium then being produced.

During this period the Salinas Valley's agricultural output did not go unnoticed as an important part of the war effort. Sugar was again rationed as thousands of tons were needed, not only for food for the Allied war effort, but also for the manufacture of industrial alcohol. The global conflict had the effect of opening up traditionally male factory work at the Spreckels Sugar plant to women, as men were inducted into military service. Fears of sabotage due to the refinery's proximity to the

During World War II the American Red Cross set up production rooms in the Salinas Valley, where first aid supplies were assembled for overseas shipment. Clean bandages were in short supply and were fabricated by hand. Courtesy, Monterey County Library

During World War II and in the years immediately following, mostly women were employed in shed work. This photo of the D'Arrigo Brothers packing shed in Castroville illustrates the work force. Photo by Larry Harmon. Courtesy, Pat Hathaway Photographs

coast necessitated night-guarding of the plant. During 1943 alone, the Spreckels Sugar Company refinery in Salinas had a daily capacity of 5,000 tons of sugar beets with an annual value of over $3.5 million.

The contributions of the Salinas Valley agriculturally during the war are perhaps best illustrated by the magnitude of the industry. The Spreckels refinery was the largest in the world. The output of the area's vegetable harvest ranked it as the world's largest producer with an annual value of nearly $67 million. The Salinas Valley had the world's largest food dehydration plant (it was government-run solely for the war effort). And

the Salinas Valley had the greatest commercial ice output in the nation. To keep production at maximum output, organized labor and the Grower-Shipper Vegetable Association agreed to arbitrate all disputes with the U.S. Conciliation Service through the war years.

The total payroll involved with agricultural production in the Salinas Valley supported over 12,000 individuals. It is no small wonder that the Salinas Valley attracted more than 56,000 new residents by the end of the 1940s.

The city of Salinas physically grew by nearly 300 acres as it annexed additional land into its city limits. The towns of Gonzales and Greenfield

In the Salinas Valley during World War II, women filled jobs traditionally held by men. Agricultural operations, such as those at the Spreckels Sugar Company Refinery and in produce sheds such as the Spiegel Foods plant shown here, could not have operated during the war without women in the work force. After the war, women continued to play a major role in the Valley's agricultural output. Courtesy, Monterey County Library

Above: At the end of World War II, Salinas once again bustled with a population supported by agricultural prosperity. Most of the downtown business district in Salinas is visible in this photograph. Courtesy, Denzil and Jennie Verardo

Above: The Salinas Valley helped feed the nation during World War II. It ranked as the world's largest producer of table vegetables with an annual output value of nearly $67 million. Courtesy, Monterey County Library

were both incorporated in 1947 due to the growing number of residents in those communities. Farther south, the Valley bustled when, in 1947, exploratory oil wells were drilled near San Ardo. The search for petroleum had begun in the southern Salinas Valley as early as 1888, and oil seeps had prompted further exploration, but the 1947 San Ardo oil discovery was the first of major importance. By the 1960s the San Ardo oil field was the sixth largest producer in California. Between 1947 and the mid-1960s the area's total production of gas and oil was valued at over $232 million with 146 million barrels of oil removed. During the same period, in 1948, the Pacific Gas and Electric Company chose Moss Landing as the site for a $90-million steam-powered generating plant, one of the largest of its type in the West.

But in the postwar period of the late 1940s, it was still agriculture that accounted for the major portion of the Salinas Valley's economy, with lettuce as the area's leading crop. The perishable nature of lettuce had limited its market expansion, but Salinas still competed well because it could grow that crop continuously for an incredible eight months a year. Then a technological breakthrough was made that expanded markets and allowed increased production without the fear of losing the crop through processing and shipping delays.

In 1947 Rex Brunsing invented the vacuum cooling process and revolutionized the manner in which lettuce was processed. After harvesting, lettuce could now be rushed to giant vacuum coolers, where the field heat was drawn out of the heads of lettuce, reducing temperatures to near freezing. Quick-cooled shipments of lettuce would last longer, thus expanding the markets to which it could be shipped. Cardboard cartons could also now be packed in the field, eliminating the need for separate packing sheds, and reducing labor costs while increasing production.

By the end of the decade, shipments from the area went to 46 states, and the Salinas Valley became responsible for between 45 and 50 percent of the nation's total head lettuce output. Walter Colton was indeed correct in his prediction that the lands along the Salinas River may "be made perfect gardens," but he could not have imagined that these gardens could feed a nation.

Above: The reality and tragedy of war struck home as Company C of the 194th Battalion, from Salinas, fought in the bloody Pacific battles of Corregidor and Bataan. Only 46 men from Company C survived the Bataan Death March. Courtesy, Monterey County Historical Society

Below: After the war, Southern Pacific Railroad's "Daylight," which ran between San Francisco and Los Angeles, provided train service for local residents as it made regular stops at the Salinas depot. Courtesy, Monterey County Library

Rubber For The War Effort
The Salinas Valley's Unique Contribution to World War II

In 1942 newspapers reported that "Uncle Sam has launched at Salinas a great project to produce rubber from guayule, a Mexican desert shrub." With the conquest of the East Indies and British Malaya, Japan in 1942 controlled over 90 percent of the world's natural rubber supply. Synthetic rubber was produced by the United States at the time, but it was decidedly inferior to the natural product, which was now in critically short supply.

Through the years, tests had been conducted on various rubber-bearing plants. It was found that guayule yielded the same kind of rubber as Southeast Asia's *Hevea* rubber tree. Guayule contained 20 percent pure rubber that realistically lent itself to harvesting. The Intercontinental Rubber Company actually began testing and experimenting with guayule as early as 1907, realizing that their natural supply was rapidly dwindling. Through the next two decades International Rubber effectively bred the plant to produce double the original percentage of rubber, which made it economically feasible in competition with other sources.

Harvesting guayule required that the entire shrub be taken, roots and all, necessitat-

ing constant new plantings after a cutting. Once harvested, guayule was cleaned and chopped in the field and sent to a mill. The chopped material was crushed between revolving steel tubes to break down the plant fibers and release rubber particles. The entire mass was then put in a water-filled tank, where the wood fiber would become waterlogged and sink, while the rubber remained floating on the top. After collecting and cleaning the rubber, it was compressed into molds for shipment.

In 1926 the Intercontinental Rubber Company began commercial operations on a large scale in the Salinas Valley. Before long, Intercontinental Rubber had nearly 8,000 acres under cultivation with 7,000 to 8,000 plants per acre, and was turning out as much as five tons of guayule rubber daily. By 1927 rubber tires were produced from guayule rubber; the company received a letter from Thomas Edison stating that he had a set he had tested and found satisfactory for 14,000 miles.

In 1930 Intercontinental Rubber's vice president, Dr. David Spence, published a paper on the cultivation of rubber in the United States. The paper outlined the perils of dependency on foreign sup-

plies. Spence also contacted the United States War Department concerning the feasibility of domestic rubber production and informed them of Intercontinental's efforts in the Salinas Valley. The War Department sent two majors, Van B. Wilkes and one whose name would be more familiar in later years, Dwight D. Eisenhower, to report on the Salinas operation and the feasibility of large-scale production.

While Eisenhower and Wilkes' report was positive, nothing was done by the government until after the outbreak of hostilities with Japan. When U.S. rubber sources were cut off, the government acted. On March 5, 1942, the Emergency Rubber Project Act was passed and the federal government took over Intercontinental's Salinas Valley operations, creating the Guayule Rubber Project. Administration of the project was put in the hands of the United States Forest Service. By April the Forest Service had sown 22,000 pounds of guayule seed in a 750-acre area in the Salinas Valley. The Forest Service hoped to get enough seedlings from this planting to put some 75,000 acres into guayule rubber production. Nurseries were also established near Bakersfield, Indio, and Ocean-

In February 1928 the Intercontinental Rubber Company manufactured the first tire made from guayule rubber. Thomas Edison endorsed one set of tires he had tested and found satisfactory for 14,000 miles. This photo was part of an Intercontinental publicity ad release. Courtesy, Monterey County Library

side, California, as well as in New Mexico, Arizona, and Texas. Within a year 30,000 seedbeds had grown enough seedlings to plant 200,000 additional acres, all of which were to be processed through the Salinas plant.

In the Salinas Valley itself the Forest Service had a technical staff of 50 and living quarters for 1,000 of its 2,000 laborers. New equipment was developed to facilitate planting on a mass scale, and to collect seed.

By the spring of 1944, 32,000 acres were devoted to the growing of guayule. In the meantime, synthetic rubber processing plants were established in the United States to turn out substitute rubber and limited amounts of natural rubber were shipped from South America.

With the end of World War II, the renewed availabiiity of Southeast Asian rubber, and the improving quality of synthetic rubber, the guayule project was discontinued. The last pound of rubber from the Valley was produced on December 14, 1945. Remaining guayule plants were dug up and burned and much of the land was planted in more profitable crops such as lettuce.

The importance of guayule and the Salinas Valley's prominent role in its production has been nearly forgotten. However, for a time during World War II, nationwide attention was focused on the Salinas Valley and its successful rubber manufacturing effort.

CHAPTER SEVEN

Back to an Agricultural Future

Everything seems to expand and prosper in the Salinas Valley. Blessed by a moderate climate and fertile soil, agriculture remains the economic mainstay of this area.

—1987-1988 Salinas Chamber of Commerce Business and Membership Directory

Many Salinas Valley communities hold festivals to celebrate their particular agricultural specialty. The oldest of these is the Castroville Artichoke Festival, begun in 1959. As the county's official vegetable, the artichoke has inspired not only respect and recipes, but runners as well. Here we see the start of the Artichoke Festival 10K run. Courtesy, Castroville Artichoke Festival Committee

"El Cortito," the short-handled hoe, was used by farm workers for more than three decades in the Salinas Valley. Banning its use was one early issue for the UFWOC, though it was not outlawed until 1974. Photo by Alexander Lowry. Courtesy, Alexander Lowry

Despite the Salinas Valley's agricultural potential, the strikes of the 1930s bitterly divided local growers and laborers in the years that followed. With the outbreak of World War II, growers welcomed the 1942 treaty with Mexico that provided "braceros" for agricultural labor. Braceros were Mexican nationals who could be brought in to alleviate the shortage of laborers that the war effort would create. The agreement included the provision that a work contract be concluded between the grower and the laborer hired; the U.S. government would pay transportation costs to and from Mexico.

The program proved successful. The lure of a better life working in the United States, however, also attracted tens of thousands of Mexican citizens who illegally crossed the border and who came to be derogatorily called "wetbacks." Congress, in order to satisfy the American growers' demand for cheap labor and to check the continuing influx of Mexicans who came illegally in search of work, in 1951 passed Public Law 78, creating a permanent bracero system for importing labor from Mexico.

In the Salinas Valley the bracero program became an essential component of agriculture. Not only did the growers have a source of inexpensive labor, but they did not have to fear repetition of the labor strife of the 1930s in the fields—braceros would not be organized. The program also facilitated the changeover from the shed packing to the field packing of lettuce and led to the use of the new vacuum cooling process. Although field packing was more labor intensive, utilization of braceros who earned less than the unionized shed workers made cost savings possible. By 1959 braceros made up 72 percent of the seasonal labor force in Monterey County.

In 1964 Public Law 78 was rescinded at the insistence of organized labor and U.S. Secretary of Labor Williard Wirtz. There were fears in the Salinas Valley that this action would create a labor shortage, with the resultant high consumer prices caused by increased production costs. Students were recruited for summer field work, but for the most part, Mexican nationals continued to be the primary source of field labor.

At the same time, in the San Joaquin Valley, Cesar Chavez was urging farm workers to unite under the red and black banner of the United Farm Workers Organizing Committee (UFWOC). Farm workers, considered by large labor unions to be not worth the effort of organization, found a champion in Chavez, who urged them to join the fight, *La Causa,* for better wages, better working and living conditions, and better opportunities for their children. While his initial efforts were focused on table-grape growers, Chavez was developing tactics that would bring industry-wide changes to agricultural labor relations.

On July 27, 1970, the United Farm Workers Union (as the UFWOC was also known) signed a contract with Giumarra Brothers in Delano, ending both the national boycott of grapes and the five-year struggle between the growers and the union, and bringing 85 percent of California's table grapes under the UFWOC label.

On that same day, the Grower-Shipper Vegetable Association of Salinas announced that 30 of its members had signed contracts with the Western Conference of Teamsters, authorizing the Teamsters to act as agents in the organization of their field workers. Cesar Chavez is reported to have responded, "This is a stab in the back. Pack your bags, we're going to Salinas." Opening salvos had been fired.

Chavez marched to Salinas. On August 3 a strike in the fields was called by the UFWOC. Nine days later headlines in the *Salinas Californian* announced, "TEAMSTERS, CHAVEZ AGREE; Farm Peace Foreseen by Historic Signing." The agreement gave the UFWOC jurisdiction over all field workers while the Western Conference of Teamsters would represent the workers in canneries, frozen food processing plants, and warehouses, as well as the truck drivers. "Farm Peace" was short-lived in the Valley, however. On August 21 growers vowed to honor their contracts with the Teamsters. By August 24 the UFWOC had closed down 31 firms. The Federal Market News Service reported that only Bud Antle, which since 1961 had a contract with the Teamsters union covering its field workers; Interharvest, which would four days later open talks with Chavez; and Sears of Watsonville were working.

By September 17 the Salinas Valley had been turned upside down. The day before, Superior Court Judge Anthony Brazil ruled that the strike was a jurisdictional dispute between the UFWOC and the Teamsters and ordered a halt to picketing on 30 Salinas Valley ranches. On September 17 the battleground was expanded as Chavez announced a 64-city national boycott of non-UFWOC harvested lettuce. Declaring that the boycott was his union's most powerful nonviolent weapon, he vowed to continue it "until the last lettuce grower is signed." Since that time, labor peace has only sporadically returned to the Salinas Valley.

Perhaps more significant than the chronological events of the 1970-1971 strike were the changes in Salinas Valley agriculture that led to it. Until the 1960s most of the farming in the Valley was locally controlled. Although the Grower-Shipper Vegetable Association, founded in 1930, provided the organization for farmers to "work toward solving labor, transportation and supply problems," its members retained their independence and their Salinas Valley focus. A change occurred when United Fruit Company bought up farms in the area and created Interharvest Inc. It was soon joined by the Purex Corporation's Freshpict Foods Inc. and by Pic N Pac, whose parent company, S.S. Pierce, was headquartered in Boston. By 1970 the Dow Chemical Company owned 17,000 acres and some 15 percent of the stock of Bud Antle Inc. While local growers and

their supporters charged that these corporations did not care about what happened in the Salinas Valley, and that Boston, home to United Fruit as well as to the Pierce Company, was selling out the area, the UFWOC targeted the parent companies as part of their boycott efforts. Local growers, whose existence depended on events in the Valley, seem to have felt betrayed by these corporate giants. Farming, after all, was just a small portion of the diverse activities of the corporations, and early settlement with the UFWOC was more attractive than a national boycott of their products, which could prove devastating.

Although the bracero program ended in 1964, local growers had been slow in responding to the changes which seemed inevitable in the farm labor situation. In October 1970 Herb Fleming, president of the Grower-Shipper Vegetable Association, in a talk to the Western Growers Association, placed part of the blame for farm labor strife on the growers themselves. Reflecting on the strike in the Salinas Valley that summer he said, "We (the growers) are now faced with revolution instead of evolution and most of it is our fault." In holding on too long to the bracero pro-

gram he felt that growers had "used excuses that they had to employ people with limited skills, that the unskilled were dumped on agriculture, that the people we employed could not manage their own lives." The image that many growers sought to project was one of benevolence, of landowners providing for the needs of the poor and uneducated laborers working for them. That image was tarnished in the world's eyes when Cesar Chavez, jailed in Salinas for as long as it took him to call off the boycott on Bud Antle lettuce, was visited by such national figures as Ethel Kennedy, Coretta King, and George McGovern. Much to the chagrin of the Citizen's Committee, the courts had created a martyr, and he was on the other side. Although Chavez was released soon after, national attention had been focused on the plight of the farm worker, and on the UFWOC and its lettuce boycott.

While tensions continued between Valley growers and the UFWOC, the Teamsters became involved in a major crisis in 1973 when their produce truck drivers went on strike for 19 days, result-

In 1968 the Pacific Gas and Electric Company completed a $132-million expansion of its Moss Landing Power Plant (shown here before construction began). Two new taller stacks joined these three to make the facility a landmark on the Central Coast, as it became the largest thermal power plant west of the Mississippi River. Courtesy, Salinas Chamber of Commerce

ing in a $36.8-million loss to the industry. Labor unrest continued to plague the Valley. In 1975 the State Agricultural Labor Relations Board (ALRB) was created, establishing more firmly the influence of outside forces on the local agricultural labor situation. Permanent resolution to agricultural labor relations in the area has yet to become a reality.

The decade of the 1960s also brought industrial changes to the Valley. After heated debate the County approved the Firestone Company's plans to build a tire production plant south of the city of Salinas in 1963. It was soon joined by Peter Paul, Inc., and Schilling-McCormick Com-

pany. There had been some industry in the Valley since 1898, when Claus Spreckels opened his sugar mill near Salinas, but most, like Spreckels Sugar, Salinas Valley Wax Paper, Smuckers, the Nestle Company, Cochran Equipment, and Growers Frozen Food, were related to agriculture. Certainly Kaiser Refractories' plant in Moss Landing was an exception, but Firestone's arrival marked the first heavy-industry development of former agricultural lands. The tire manufacturing plant soon became one of the Valley's largest employers with 1,800 local positions. And unlike agricultural employment, these jobs were permanent and year-round.

In order to maintain the delicate balance between industry and agriculture, the Monterey County Industrial Development Corporation had been established in 1952. By 1971 a Salinas newspaper editorial would lament its passing and issue

the call to "get back into the highly competitive business of recruiting COMPATIBLE industry for our area." In the 1970s the Monterey County Board of Supervisors established the Overall Economic Development Commission to be "the principal coordinator of the various local activities designed to stimulate new private and public investment and provide permanent employment and growth opportunities" in the county. The commission was joined in these activities by the Economic Development Corporation of Monterey County (formed in 1983) and by area chambers of commerce, and together they began working to en-

For almost two decades the Firestone Tire and Rubber Company plant south of Salinas was the Valley's largest industrial facility. After tire production ceased in 1980, efforts began to find new tenants for the massive facility. Courtesy, Salinas Chamber of Commerce

Above: The Salinas Fire Department made good use of this station before it was outfitted with a new main station in the 1980s. Photo by Denzil Verardo. Courtesy, Denzil and Jennie Verardo

Facing page, top and bottom: During the last three decades change has been a key word in the city of Salinas. City hall was demolished and replaced with modern offices and a city council rotunda adjoined by a new Public Safety Building, all on Lincoln Avenue. Photo by Jennie Verardo. Courtesy, Denzil and Jennie Verardo

sure economic stability locally by maintaining an environment conducive to both agriculture and industrial development.

The city of Salinas grew in 1963 when it annexed the Alisal area east of the city. Attempts had been made as early as 1949 to bring this area into Salinas. When the annexation was completed on August 5, 1963, the population of Salinas went from 31,000 to almost 50,000, and its area increased by almost one-fourth.

While some South Valley communities remained static during this period, others like King City realized impressive gains. In 1966 alone, King City grew by 300 people, a 10 percent increase in population. The population growth was accompanied by a 76 percent increase in the valuation of building permits over the previous year. While there was some industrial development, most of the growth was in the agricultural sector. In 1963 Paul Masson and Mirassou planted vineyards near Soledad, and, as other wine producers joined them, a major economic impact would be felt in the South Valley, especially in the Gonzales area. In the early 1970s the Prudential Insurance Company developed what would come to be considered the largest contiguous wine-producing property in the free world. The San Bernabe Vineyard comprised 12,600 acres near King City.

In spite of this economic growth, the Salinas Valley remained predominantly agricultural. In 1966, with a $175-million gross farm income, Monterey County ranked eighth among agricultural counties in California and 11th in the United States. Ten years later lettuce alone was a $155.7-million crop. Despite labor problems and

This page: The Carnegie Library, also known as the Salinas Public Library (below), on Main and San Luis streets, was replaced by the John Steinbeck Library on Lincoln and San Luis streets in April 1960. Courtesy, Denzil and Jennie Verardo

concern that increased development might turn the Salinas area into "another San Jose," the Valley prospered during the 1960s and 1970s.

This prosperity seemed threatened with the opening of a new decade. In June 1980 the Firestone Company ceased operations at their Salinas plant. The next year Peter Paul Cadbury pulled out. In 1982 the venerable Spreckels Sugar Company ceased refining operations. The industrial development that had seemed so promising had in the end produced empty manufacturing plants and massive unemployment. Then in 1985, just as the Valley seemed to be pulling itself out of that situation and reestablishing some equilibrium, California Coastal Farms became the first of many produce companies to go out of business. It was soon followed by Let-U-Pak, Hansen Farms, Veg-Co, Harden Farms, Veg-Pak, and

West Coast Farms, all within a one-year period. In addition, Paul Masson Vineyards in Soledad was closed by its parent company, Seagram Wine Company, pulling 1,800 acres out of production and putting 144 employees out of work.

But the Valley would prove its resilience. New companies were attracted to begin rebuilding the industrial/commercial sector, and little permanent damage had apparently been done to the agricultural industry as a whole. In 1987, for the third time, gross farm receipts in the county topped one billion dollars. While lettuce remained the leading crop, with the Salinas Valley producing 80 percent of the nation's summer head lettuce, Ed Angstadt, president of the Grower-Shipper Vegetable Association, stated in 1988 that "the

In the midst of growth and change, the need to preserve Salinas Valley's heritage became felt. In 1974 a group of civic-minded women who shared an interest in gourmet cooking opened John Steinbeck's birthplace as a luncheon restaurant. The Steinbeck House, preserved by the Valley Guild, has added thousands of dollars to local charities. Courtesy, Salinas Chamber of Commerce

ability to produce a wide variety of produce and commodities has allowed the Valley to remain prosperous." This variety included broccoli, celery, strawberries, mushrooms, nursery stock, cauliflower, wine grapes, asparagus, fruit and nut crops, tomatoes, and the county's official vegetable, the artichoke.

The future bodes well for the Salinas Valley. Foresight provided for the construction of two water conservation and flood control dams on the Salinas River in the South Valley— Nacimiento Dam, built in 1957, and San Antonio Dam, built in 1964. And future sources of agricultural and domestic water supplies are being investigated. Sewage facilities are being upgraded in the Salinas-Castroville area through participation in the Monterey Regional Water Pollution Control Agency, while air quality is monitored and maintained by the Monterey Bay Unified Air Pollution Control District. A county general plan assures

the maintenance of a quality environment and controlled compatible growth in unincorporated areas. These same assurances are being addressed in the incorporated communities by the city councils.

In the end, at least for the foreseeable future, it all comes back to the land—to the natural environment of the Salinas Valley, transformed over the years from a barren plain to one of the most productive agricultural areas in the world. Today the focus seems to be on the protection of the incredible resources here—clean air, clean and abundant water, fertile soil, and open space.

Salinas Valley people seem to have a sense of this fertile place. It has made them distinctive, perhaps more centered, more closely tied to the miracles of nature. Honesty, trust, dependability, and loyalty—these are qualities respected and ex-

Above: Progress was accelerated in local higher education in the 1970s and 1980s. Hartnell College witnessed new construction in 1974 with this athletic facility. The Olympic-sized pool features sculptures and was the largest solar-heated pool in the world at the time of construction. Courtesy, Jerome Kasavan Associates

Facing page: Main Street became "Oldtown Salinas" in 1980, and the four-lane thoroughfare was beautified with trees, red brick crosswalks, and the restoration and rejuvenation of many buildings. Photo by Denzil Verardo. Courtesy, Denzil and Jennie Verardo

Facing page: Fine art development was given a further boost in the Salinas Valley with the completion of the Hartnell College Visual Arts facility in 1978. Photo by Ron Starr. Courtesy, Jerome Kasavan Associates

Above: The new Community Center building adjacent to the California Rodeo Grounds was graced in 1982 with a unique sculpture by Claus Oldenburg. The striking Community Center serves a multipurpose function as a meeting, theater, and conference facility. Courtesy, Salinas Chamber of Commerce

pected in people here. Expectations are generally realistic and most often realized—people know what they want and work hard to achieve it. And their triumphs and struggles are all played out against a background of rich brown soil and blue sky, in a valley that resembles a verdant patchwork made up of crops to feed a hungry world.

The majesty of nature is evident in this Pinnacles landscape. Photo by John Elk III

The Valley possesses riches almost beyond measure—in its people, who are willing to work to realize their dreams, and in its natural environment, which has been a key to those dreams. For you see, from the low-lying fields of artichokes near the mouth of the Salinas River, down through the bright green rows of lettuce and the golden pasturage to the acres of vineyards, alfalfa, and broccoli in the south, the wealth of the Salinas Valley has long been its agricultural resources—its green gold.

Above: This sparse oak forest appears along a backcountry road near King City. Photo by Lee Foster

Right: A Shooting Star Dodecatheon brightens this Salinas Valley field. Photo by Lee Foster

Enthusiastic participants of the grape stomp, at the Mission Wine Festival in Soledad, keep on top of their work. Photo by Lee Foster

An adventurous cowboy tests his skill in the Brahma Bull Riding event during the California Rodeo. Photo by Alexander Lowry

Left: These flowers sweeten the path to Mission Nuestra Senora de Soledad. Photo by John Elk III

Facing page: The Steinbeck House in Salinas has many stories to tell visitors. Photo by Mark E. Gibson

Below: This nineteenth-century Victorian home graciously greets the viewer. Photo by John Elk III

These young lettuce "line up" smartly in a field near King City. Photo by Alexander Lowry

Left: These farm workers ensure the success of the cauliflower harvest. Photo by Lee Foster

Below: This Salinas cauliflower is ripe for the picking. Photo by Mark E. Gibson

Above: The bell pepper harvest is seen in all its green glory from on high. Photo by Alexander Lowry

Right: Brussel sprouts luxuriously carpet the Salinas Valley. Photo by Lee Foster

Facing Page: A red barn provides the background for these equally colorful products of the Gizdich Fruit Farm. Photo by Lee Foster

Derricks doggedly toil in oil fields at San Ardo. Photo by Alexander Lowry

Irrigation pipes such as these have enabled agriculture to flourish in the Salinas Valley. Photo by John Elk III

*Above: This aerial view shows the scale of the La Cienega red wines winery of Almaden.
Photo by Lee Foster*

Center: In the Jekel vineyards in Greenfield, a cluster of Pinot Noir grapes ripens toward a cultured future. Photo by Alexander Lowry

Below: These Almaden vineyards are brought to fruition with the help of overhead sprinkler irrigation. Photo by Lee Foster

Partners in Progress

The Salinas Valley has seen many changes in the 200 years since Portola and his small, ragged band of Spanish explorers emerged onto its fertile lands from the foothills of the treacherous Santa Lucia mountains. But as "Partners in Progress" throughout the Valley's development, local entrepreneurs, farmers, and business owners have provided leadership in all facets of community life.

Originally dominated by big, landholding rancheros, the Salinas Valley first gained economic prominence as a cattle-producing region. Later, using newly built dams and irrigation ditches, tenant farmers prospered by raising beans and sugar beets on land where herds of cattle once grazed.

Lettuce, of course, eventually surpassed beans, beets, and cattle as the Salinas Valley's number one crop. But artichokes, too, became an important commercial produce item as Italian farmers filled the cool, foggy fields to the north with row upon row of the spiky, green vegetable.

By the 1950s men had returned to shed work in significant numbers. However, women continued to play an important role in the packing operations. Courtesy, Richard Verardo

As the vegetable-growing industry and its related enterprises took over the local economy, the Valley became known as "The Salad Bowl of the World." And the Salinas Valley continues to reign as the world's leading producer of fresh vegetables.

Though still firmly rooted in agriculture, the economy of the Salinas Valley today is also fueled by a diverse and growing business community. From related agricultural industries such as packing and shipping, to real estate development, construction, retail, restaurants, schools, hospitals, and professional services, Salinas Valley business owners are deeply involved in the community at large, promoting the health and vitality of the entire region.

In fact, "involvement" is a common theme running through these stories of local enterprises. For the business owners of the Salinas Valley have never stood apart from the rest of the community. As true "Partners in Progress," they continue to play a vital role in the ongoing development of the region.

The organizations whose stories are detailed on the following pages have chosen to support this important literary and civic project. They illustrate the variety of ways in which individuals and their businesses have contributed to the area's growth and development. The civic involvement of Salinas Valley businesses, institutions of learning, and government in cooperation with its citizens has made the area an excellent place to live and work.

SALINAS AREA CHAMBER OF COMMERCE

While most professional associations have very narrow interests, focusing on the needs and concerns of a single industry, chambers of commerce represent a very broad constituency of business owners.

The effect of that important difference can be clearly seen in the mission statement of the Salinas Area Chamber of Commerce, which states the organization's commitment "to represent and assist the business community of the Salinas area in the development and pursuit of goals and programs which will improve the economic well-being of the citizens and preserve and improve the quality of life."

The first City of Salinas Chamber of Commerce was founded in 1918 by a group of Salinas Valley business owners. The organization's first president was local

The Salinas Area Chamber of Commerce moved into the newly remodeled Salinas Valley Savings and Loan building at 119 East Alisal Street in 1961.

businessman John Souza, now deceased.

The Salinas chamber later merged with the Monterey County Chamber of Commerce and, when the City of Salinas annexed the City of Alisal in 1963, with the Alisal Chamber of Commerce.

In 1961 the chamber moved its offices into the newly remodeled Salinas Valley Savings and Loan building at 119 East Alisal Street, which houses the organization today.

Over its 70-year history the Salinas Area Chamber of Commerce has developed a philosophy of aggressive participation in the local community. With an emphasis on helping people recognize and appreciate the relationship between business and the prosperity of a community, the chamber has established a number of community-oriented programs.

The chamber was the lead agency sponsoring the first Monterey Bay Economic Outlook Conference in 1987. Its Leadership Sali-

nas program, begun in 1982, provides in-depth, personal leadership training for future community leaders and is considered one of the best programs of its kind on the Central Coast. And a major portion of the chamber's efforts is devoted to providing management training for local small business owners and managers.

From its founding, the Salinas Area Chamber of Commerce has employed a professional staff that works full time promoting Salinas business. The staff is well-known for providing visitors with information about the Salinas area, and also assists inquiring industries with demographics, site investigation, and other information they will need to locate in the area. And the staff coordinates chamber committee activities, events, and programs; provides alternatives and direction to business owners and managers; and publishes printed material on the community.

The chamber is also the only organization of its kind in the state of California that provides its members with access to a credit union.

The Salinas Area Chamber of Commerce, through its commitment to its membership and its community, has developed a statewide reputation as a dynamic and productive organization. With a current membership of more than 1,300 businesses and professionals, the chamber continues to promote the economic well-being of the community, working every day to help local businesses prosper.

CITY OF SALINAS

nearly 100,000, making Salinas one of California's fastest-growing cities. For the 10-year period from 1978 to 1988 the city's annual growth rate averaged nearly 3 percent. Nearly half of Monterey County's total growth has occurred in Salinas.

Fortunately for its citizens, the growth of Salinas has been accompa-

In 1887 Salinas was a cattle town with gas street-lights and an unpaved Main Street (left). Pictured below is the same view, looking north on Main Street from Alisal Street. Today Salinas is a growing community with a population of more than 100,000. Photo (left), courtesy, Monterey County Historical Society. Photo (below) by Kevin Clement

When Elias Howe acquired 80 acres of land inside the bend of the big slough Sanjon del Alisal in 1856, he probably never envisioned his new property as the nucleus of a sprawling, spirited city. But 132 years later, with a population exceeding 100,000, the 11,000-acre city of Salinas has become the economic and agricultural capital of an entire region.

Located at the north end of the long Salinas Valley and partially fringed by the Gavilan Mountains, Salinas was originally a cattle-raising center. However, with the advent of large-scale irrigation techniques and refrigerated railcars, the city soon was surrounded by fields of vegetable crops. Today Salinas is the processing and shipping center of America's "salad bowl." During peak growing seasons more than 1,000 trucks loaded with lettuce, broccoli, cauliflower, and a host of other produce commodities leave the city daily.

In addition to its fame as a center of agriculture, Salinas is the home of the world-renowned California Rodeo and the Monterey County seat. The local leader in medical, media, and financial activities, Salinas is also the birthplace of Nobel and Pulitzer prize-winning au-

thor John Steinbeck.

The city was incorporated in 1874 by 112 of the community's 150 qualified voters. Salinas is self-governing with a city council/city manager form of management. The city council consists of six council members elected by district and a mayor elected at large for a four-year term. Since the members and the mayor are not full-time officials, the council appoints a city manager as its administrative agent to carry out its policies and directives.

By 1950 the population of Salinas had reached nearly 14,000. During the next 30 years that figure would increase dramatically to

nied by thoughtful and creative planning. Looking ahead 20 years from 1988, the Salinas General Plan focuses on the city's long-range physical development while the city's Office of Economic Development keeps the local economy vital by attracting new businesses.

The council and employees of the City of Salinas are dedicated to improving the quality of life for every citizen. The city's mission statement, "People serving people for a better community," serves as a reminder of the commitment to excellence and the tradition of community spirit that began in Salinas' first century and continues into its second.

AUSONIO CONSTRUCTION INC.

Andy Ausonio built his first house while he was still in high school in the late 1940s. It was a two-unit, one-bedroom duplex on Koester Street in Castroville, and it took him nearly two years to complete.

Since that time Ausonio Construction has built more than 1,000 residential, commercial, and industrial structures throughout the Central Coast, including the Barnyard Shopping Center in Carmel; the enormous Castroville Cold Storage building, which covers 2.5 acres under one roof; and the sprawling Castroville Industrial Park.

Ausonio was born on the Mulligan Hill artichoke ranch near the mouth of the Salinas River, the only son of hardworking Italian immigrants. He attended high school in

Shown here before completion is Ausonio Construction's first project—a duplex on Koester Street, built in 1947.

Salinas and later graduated from Hartnell College.

In the fall of 1951 Ausonio went to work as an operating engineer at the Pacific Gas and Electric Power Plant in Moss Landing. That same year the Korean War broke out and, as a member of the National Guard, he went on to active duty.

PG&E held Ausonio's job open for him until he returned to Castroville after his service. He continued to serve as a National Guard captain while working for the utility company. He also began moonlighting as a builder.

In 1964 Ausonio finally quit his job at PG&E and gave his budding construction venture his full attention. Since he had been working at it on a part-time basis for years, he already had an experienced, three-man crew in place. He concentrated his early efforts on developing residential and rental property, but eventually he focused on commercial construction.

One of Ausonio Construction's largest commercial projects, the Castroville Industrial Park, is the site of the corporation's new offices. Prior to 1988, when the offices were moved, Ausonio and his wife, Nancy, had operated the company from offices in the back of their Castroville home.

The couple's son, civil engineer Andrew Ausonio, Jr., joined his father's construction company in 1988. Daughter Diane Ausonio

Andy Ausonio proudly displays the handsome bronze 1988 Excellence in Construction Award presented to Ausonio Construction by the Associated General Contractors of California.

Ausonio Construction's enduring commitment to excellence in building is seen in the new Monterey Federal Credit Union Building.

works for Nancy Ausonio's company, Pacific Construction, as a job coordinator and estimator. The couple's youngest daughter, Linda Ausonio, is a schoolteacher at Castroville school.

Ausonio is one of the founders of the Bank of Salinas, where he serves as chairman of the board. He also serves on the board of the Salinas Community Hospital and is on the board of directors of the Associated General Contractors of California (AGC).

In 1988 Ausonio's firm was honored by the AGC for its work preparing Laguna Seca Raceway for the 1987 visit of Pope John Paul II. Among other things contributed to the project, Ausonio's company built a massive altar platform in the shape of a cross, constructed a towering cross that had to withstand 100-mile-per-hour winds, graded a path 60 feet wide and

1,400 feet long connecting the bases of the two crosses for the placement of 125,000 potted petunias—and then dismantled it all at the end of the visit.

Even with all his accomplishments, Andy Ausonio remembers his beginnings. He still owns that first duplex he built during his

high school days. It serves as a reminder of the hard work that helped make Ausonio Construction Inc. one of the leading building contractors in the Salinas Valley.

The Sakata Seed Company building, which serves as the international firm's American seed research and sales center, illustrates Ausonio Construction's diversity and quality work.

HARTNELL COLLEGE

Hartnell College is very nearly the oldest community college in California. And though its founding dates back to 1920, the roots of this venerable institution are buried in a previous century.

In 1828 William Edward Petty Hartnell first stepped ashore in Monterey. The English linguist had come to California, then a Mexican territory, as a trading agent for a group of Peruvian merchants. He struck a deal for his employers with the local missions to trade hides and tallow for money and finished goods. He was so impressed with the beautiful country, however, that he didn't return with the ship, but instead settled on the Central Coast.

Hartnell soon converted to Catholicism and married Maria Theresa de la Guerra, the 14-year-old daughter of the famous Santa Barbara family. He later gave up trading altogether and became a naturalized citizen of Mexico. As such, he received a land grant of 48,000 acres. In 1833 Hartnell used a section of his new rancho near

This panther statue (pictured here in front of the former Salinas Junior College) was designed by Raymond Puccinelli in 1940 as part of the WPA (Works Progress Administration) art program.

the Gabilan foothills to construct the first school of higher learning in California.

Hartnell's Colegio de San Jose consisted of two adobe buildings constructed by Indian converts trained by the Catholic padres. One long, two-story structure housed a dormitory, with a master's room upstairs and study rooms below. The other, smaller building, set on the banks of the Alisal Creek, provided the dining room and kitchen. Both buildings had glass windows—the first ever in the area.

The first students traveled to the school on horseback and in ox-carts from as far away as Mexico. Fifteen boys registered and boarded at the college the first year. They were charged $200 apiece and were taught Latin, mathematics, and philosophy by Hartnell and two Jesuit priests.

The school was closed after only two years because of lack of students. Hartnell never reopened it, content to busy himself with his own children, his ranch, and his adopted community.

In 1920 the board of trustees of the Salinas Union High School District founded Salinas Junior College. The school was well attended and eventually moved to its present location on Homestead Avenue in 1936. The name was changed to Hartnell College 11 years later.

The Hartnell College Community College District was organized one year later, and today Hartnell College enrolls more than 7,000 students in both day and evening classes. The institution offers a two-year program and awards the Associate of Arts and Sciences degrees, as well as a variety of certificate programs. It also provides vocational training and continuing education classes, in addition to cultural and recreational activities for the community.

Through the years Hartnell College has responded to the diverse and changing educational needs of its community with a variety of programs and services. The Hartnell Community Education Program provides a number of courses for continuing education. It offers in-service computer and management training for employees of community businesses, and an extensive youth program, including Hartnell for Kids, Hartnell College Youth Ballet, and the Conservatory of Music and Fine Arts.

The college has expanded its service to South County through the Gleason Center, which was established in 1987 in King City through the bequest of Villeroy Gleason, former trustee of the college. The Gleason home has been converted to an educational center where students can

The original adobe building that housed William Hartnell's Colegio de San Jose was also fitted with the first glass window in California. Photo circa 1940

ater in the region. In addition to being a full-service theater serving the Hartnell College Community College District and Monterey County, the Western Stage is a full-time vocational training program in theater arts for actors and technicians. It is one of the most outstanding training programs at the community college level in the country.

Hartnell College has an enrollment of more than 7,000 students, and offers programs and services tailored to the needs of the Salinas Valley community.

now complete most requirements for the transfer degree.

In the spring of 1985 Hartnell College and 12 Salinas Valley public and private high schools formed the High School/Hartnell Coordinating Council for the purpose of sharing resources and reducing duplication of education.

The Hartnell College Planetarium is the only one in Monterey County, serving area residents and more than 2,000 grammar school students annually with educational lectures and shows.

Hartnell serves the business community in a variety of ways. Computer information system students assist organizations by evaluating their computer management systems. The Pace Program provides businesses throughout the community with individually tailored, computerized exercise programs for their employees. The Hartnell internship program gives students a chance to gain real-world work experience di-

rectly related to their areas of study, while giving employers the opportunity to assess students as possible permanent employees.

The Western Stage consistently produces some of the finest live the-

A century and a half after William Hartnell founded his tiny college in the Gabilan foothills, Hartnell College carries on a proud tradition of community-based learning.

JOHN SNOW SEED COMPANY

John Snow is more than just a salesman; he is a seedsman—one whose knowledge and expertise have guided the John Snow Seed Company from a one-man operation into one of the foremost independent seed dealers in the Salinas Valley.

In 1958, when Snow first began to work in the seed business, he was a low man on someone else's totem pole. After Snow had spent a few years working in the Salinas produce industry he met V.W. Clow, the owner of a small, local seed company. Clow was looking for a new salesman and offered the position to Snow, who accepted, marking the beginning of a long association between the two men.

Snow worked hard for Clow for the next 16 years. Though he started at the bottom he advanced quickly in the organization, eventually becoming its top salesman. Snow credits much of his success during those years to Clow's tutelage, fondly recalling his employer as an "ornery old man," little interested in equipping his employees

John Snow Seed Company moved from a storage space in an old poultry-processing building to a 7,000-square-foot warehouse just south of Salinas.

with such office luxuries as desks or places to sit. He just made sure they knew the seed business inside and out.

When Clow died in 1974 Snow made an unsuccessful attempt to purchase his business. A year later, with $5,000 in start-up money (a shoestring by any standard), Snow struck out on his own.

At first, the fledgling John Snow Seed Company was no more than a storage space in an old poultry-processing building on the corner of Market and Front streets, long since razed. There was no office in the tiny warehouse so Snow had to work out of the Buick station wagon he was using to deliver seed.

Within a year Snow had hired a secretary and moved his one-man operation into a larger warehouse on Brunken Avenue. He conducted business from that location for the next 10 years. During that time he began expanding his firm's service area beyond the Salinas Valley to include the San Joaquin Valley, Huron, and Bakersfield, with some clients as far away as Yuma, Arizona, and a few overseas.

As the company grew, the nature of agriculture changed. Grow-

John Snow is one of the Salinas Valley's top seed dealers, representing 25 producers worldwide.

ers moved into the modern business world with computers, elaborate phone systems, and fax machines.

But Snow stayed on top of the changes by selling new information as well as the new products, maintaining his organization's reputation as an informed resource on which his clients could rely. He even participated with growers conducting trial plantings of new seed varieties that might prove superior to, and so replace, the unsold seed in his own warehouse.

In 1984, with his business flourishing beyond all his expectations, Snow purchased an acre of land seven miles southeast of the Salinas city limits. There he built a 7,000-square-foot warehouse. From this facility the John Snow Seed Company now represents more than 25 different seed producers worldwide and ranks among the Salinas Valley's top-grossing seed dealers.

"And all of the people who work for me," says Snow, "have a place to sit."

PACIFIC GAS & ELECTRIC COMPANY

Since 1963 the Coast Valleys Division of Pacific Gas & Electric has served the area's energy needs from this facility at 356 East Alisal Street.

Before its first gas and electric service was established in the late 1800s, the Salinas Valley was a sleepy, untilled region powered by a few mechanical water wheels and lit by oil lamps. Today the Coast Valleys Division of Pacific Gas & Electric provides light and power to more than 139,000 customers throughout Monterey and San Benito counties.

Monterey County's first gas utility was incorporated on May 4, 1875, and construction of the company's new gas plant began on land at Pajaro and Sausal streets, where the town's water plant was located. The Salinas City Gas and Water Company began immediately to extend its service throughout the community.

Eleven years later Salinas City Gas and Water added a small electric generating plant to its system. A brick and galvanized iron powerhouse was built next to the gasworks, and two 150-kilowatt generators were installed to supply power to the arc and incandescent lamps and to drive the city water system's pump.

The firm changed its name to Salinas City Light and Water Company in 1896. Two years later the utility was succeeded by the Salinas Water, Light, and Power Company.

Monterey County Gas and Electric Company purchased the Salinas utility, along with the troubled Monterey Gas and Electric Company and the rickety Monterey-Pacific Railroad in 1903. The new enterprise, formed by a group of ambitious Los Angeles investors, floundered under its absentee administration until 1906, when it was taken over by a group of San Francisco businessmen.

But the northern management was no more successful; the little system failed to generate enough revenues to pay for maintenance and operating expenses. Debt piled upon debt as small county banks from all over the state came to the rescue with $5,000 and $10,000 loans.

Then in early 1911 Frank G. Baum, a brilliant young Stanford University graduate, consulting engineer, and designer of important parts of the Pacific Gas & Electric sys-

tem, with the help of San Francisco entrepreneur W.P. Hammon, took over management of the struggling utility. The two men eventually took over the firm completely with their California Consolidated Light and Power Company.

But just one year later the New York-based holding company that operated San Francisco's streetcar system purchased a number of Monterey, Salinas, and King City utility systems, including California Consolidated, and incorporated them into the Coast Valleys Gas and Electric Company.

Over the next decade Coast Valleys fought for control of the area's utility market with its chief competitor, Midland Counties Public Service Corporation. But the movement for eventual consolidation of the gas and electric systems of Northern California was inexorable, and by 1927 Pacific Gas & Electric had acquired both companies.

Today PG&E continues to provide for that demand through facilities such as the Moss Landing Power Plant. The plant, built during the 1950s, with additional units added during the 1960s, produces 2 million kilowatts of electricity through thermal generation. Additional sources, including the geothermal power plants near Cloverdale, California, the hydrogeneration facilities in the Sierra Mountains, and the state-of-the-art Diablo Canyon Nuclear Power Plant in San Luis Obispo, provide PG&E customers with power they can depend on.

As the company shapes itself for the future with a new emphasis on service over growth, Pacific Gas & Electric's Coast Valleys Division continues to keep the lights burning in the Salinas Valley.

BELLI*CHRISTENSEN, AIA, ARCHITECTS

Belli*Christensen, AIA, Architects, is a company with a long heritage in the Salinas Valley.

Raymond Belli was born in Greenfield, California, the youngest of six children. Shortly thereafter his parents moved the family to nearby Soledad where they purchased and operated the Foley Hotel. His father died less than three years later, but his mother continued to operate the hotel through most of his youth.

Ray attended grammar school in Soledad and graduated from Gonzales High School, where he participated in student government and in all sports, including boxing. After serving for two years in the Army Air Corps he attended Salinas Junior College (currently Hartnell College).

Ray used the G.I. Bill to attend the then all-male California Polytechnic State College in San Luis Obispo. By this time he had married Francis Ricca, whom he had known in Soledad.

Ray graduated from Cal Poly with a Bachelor of Science degree

*The Austin House, current home of Belli*Christensen, AIA, Architects, was renovated by the firm in 1979. Courtesy, Marco Zecchin*

in architectural engineering. One of his teachers was George Hasselain, who later became dean of the School of Architecture. Homer Delawie, now a prominent Southern California architect, was one of his classmates. His first job after graduation was as a civilian with the Army Corps of Engineers in Alaska. Since he was one of only a handful of people taking

the professional exam in that state, he became the first licensed architect from his class.

After the birth of his first child, Ray left Alaska and returned with his young family to the Bay Area and the Salinas Valley to begin his practice. One of his first local employers was Robert Stanton, FAIA, of Carmel.

Ray practiced by himself for a year or two before joining George Fox, AIA, to form Fox and Belli, Architects. The firm's office was located at 345 Abbott Street. After many years at that location the firm joined George Kuska and became Belli, Fox and Kuska, Architects. In 1970, at Fox and Belli, Ray hired Fred Christensen, who had recently graduated from Cal Poly San Luis Obispo.

Fred's father was a Navy officer, so his childhood was spent mov-

*This cooling and shipping facility in Spreckels was designed by Belli*Christensen for Tanimura and Antle in 1987. Courtesy, Marco Zecchin*

The Krough House, renovated by Belli*Christensen, is on the National Register of Historic Places. Courtesy, Marco Zecchin

ing around the world. His family eventually settled in Mountain View, California, where he attended elementary school and high school.

Immediately after graduation from Cal Poly, Fred married Helaine Mariash, whom he had met in Mountain View. With the offer of employment he and his wife moved to Salinas where they now live with their three children.

Established in 1978, Belli*Christensen, AIA, is an 11-person firm with a diverse practice throughout Central California. Project types include schools, industrial, housing,

Above: The Rossi Building was designed in 1981 by Belli*Christensen for Emillio Rossi of Salinas. Courtesy, Marco Zecchin

Right: The First Armory Building in downtown Salinas, renovated by Belli*Christensen, was originally the National Guard Armory. Courtesy, Marco Zecchin

medical, and recreational. The company has designed facilities for the agriculture industry, including clients such as Bud of California, Tanimura and Antle, Valley Harvest, D'Arrigo Brothers, Nunes Company, Meyer Tomatoes, and many more.

The Mission School in Soledad, Lagunita School, and Gavilan View Middle School are three of the firm's most notable school de-

signs. Payless Plaza, Northridge Plaza, and Broadway Plaza in King City are three commercial projects completed by the principals. Belli*Christensen has designed or supervised more than 1,500 housing units, including Mariner Village and Cypress Village apartments.

With the advent of Old Town revitalization, the firm became actively involved in the renovation of downtown structures. The Krough House, at 146 Central Avenue, was renovated and placed on the National Register of Historic Places.

The Austin House was renovated by Belli*Christensen and became the firm's offices in 1979.

The company received two design awards in 1984 for the Krough House and Sacred Heart Church, and then again two years later for the Deen Building and the Central Avenue Apartments.

Belli*Christensen, AIA, Architects remains today a vibrant, progressive, and award-winning business. It is a company with a strong and stable past as well as a clear and optimistic future.

SALINAS VALLEY MEMORIAL HOSPITAL

The Salinas Valley Memorial Hospital opened its doors in 1953 with a post-World War II dedication ". . . to the health of the community in memory of the men and women of the armed forces who made the supreme sacrifice for their community and their nation."

Since that day Salinas Valley Memorial has remained true to its founding spirit, expanding its services, improving its facilities, and keeping pace with the needs of the community it serves.

Before the hospital was established, relatively few health services were available to Salinas Valley resi-

The Salinas Valley Memorial Hospital shown shortly after opening in the early 1950s (above), and the modern, 229-bed comprehensive medical center today (left). Dedicated to the health of the community in memory of all who have sacrificed greatly for their community and nation, the hospital continues to serve area residents with a broad range of quality medical services.

dents. At that time anyone requiring a complex medical treatment had to travel to San Jose, or even as far as San Francisco, to find a full-service medical facility.

In 1941 a group of civic-minded business and professional leaders began a campaign to raise funds for the construction of a modern hospital in the Salinas Valley. The group formed the Salinas Com-

munity Hospital Association, located a suitable building site at the southeast edge of the city, and set about trying to obtain federal assistance for the project. At that time, however, the needs of America's growing involvement in World War II put any hopes of federal aid for the hospital project on hold.

When the war ended in 1945, the Hospital Association was still work-

ing to fill the community's need for a local hospital. That year the association's directors changed the group's name to The Salinas Valley Memorial Hospital Association to honor the memory of young men from the Salinas Valley who perished during the Bataan Death March.

Blocked by the war effort from obtaining government help, and unable to generate enough money through local fund-raising drives to finance the proposed facility, the hospital association campaigned for the formation of a hospital district. In June 1947 the citizens for the community voted to form that district, and two years later local voters passed a bond issue to further fund the hospital's construction. The old hospital association was later dissolved, and all funds collected by the group were turned over to the newly formed Salinas Val-

Wielding a pick to break ground at the March 1953 ceremony is Bruce Church, a founding father of Salinas Valley Memorial Hospital.

ley Memorial Hospital District.

Construction of the hospital was finally begun in 1950. A ground-breaking ceremony was held on March 29 of that year at the East Romie site donated by former association co-chairman Bruce Church. The site had been selected by the original hospital association nearly 10 years earlier.

When the 129-bed hospital was completed three years later at a cost of $2,305,000, President Dwight D. Eisenhower sent a telegram to Church, then president of the new institution's board of directors, praising the successful project as an ". . . admirable example of local self-reliance and initiative."

Designed with growth in mind, Salinas Valley Memorial Hospital expanded its services and facilities as the surrounding community grew during the next three decades. In 1961 the hospital's pediatric facilities were enlarged. Central Supply and both the recovery and emergency rooms were expanded in 1971, and between 1973 and 1977 the Concentrated Care Unit, Nuclear Medicine Department, and general laboratory facilities were all expanded.

The Bruce Church Diagnostic Center, constructed in 1977, greatly enhanced the ability of physicians at Salinas Valley Memorial to look inside the human body without surgery. Using sophisticated equipment, such as the Magnetic Resonance Imager, the Color Flow Ultrasound Scanner, and the CT Scanner, complex medical myster-ies could now be solved without invasive procedures.

The L.M. Tynan Emergency Center, expanded in 1983, provides for immediate treatment of emergencies with state-of-the-art equipment and facilities, including a fracture room, a trauma room, a pediatric examining room, and a large waiting room. The facility's expansion also included a Paramedic Base Station, which allows E.R. physicians to supervise by radio life-saving treatment administered at the scene of faraway emergencies.

The Joyce Wyman Outpatient Surgery Center, completed in 1986, is the first facility in the area built specifically for those patients requiring simple surgical procedures that allow them to return home the same day. The center continues to provide a growing number of patients with access to the hospital's fully equipped operating rooms on an outpatient basis.

The latest addition to Salinas

Salinas Valley Memorial Hospital offers its patients responsive, professional attention in an environment that features the latest in medical technology.

Valley Memorial is the Harden Memorial Heart Center. Completed in 1987, this state-of-the-art facility is the Central Coast's first comprehensive heart treatment center. The heart center has the capacity to accommodate 500 catheterizations and 125 angioplasties annually.

Located on the patio level of the Harden Heart Center is the Francis Cislini Outpatient Plaza. Completed in the first part of 1989, the plaza is named in honor of the former publisher of what is today the

Building contractors have been busy at the hospital since the 1960s. The past three decades have seen expansion in pediatrics and recovery, and centers for diagnostics, emergency, outpatient surgery, and heart treatment have all been built.

Salinas Californian. The plaza includes a 100-seat multipurpose educational conference facility donated by the hospital's Service League. This conference facility overlooks a patio named in honor of James R. Fassett, M.D., which includes a colorful waterfall and pool, also funded by the Service League. Francis and Rosalie Cislini funded two sculptures by Emile Norman of Big Sur that are displayed in the plaza and lobby of the Harden Heart Center.

Eye surgery is performed at Salinas Valley Memorial near the plaza in the Burke-Weber Ophthalmological Center, also located on the patio level. Because of its fine reputation, the Burke-Weber Center has become the leading eye care facility for the Salinas Valley.

To help the hospital continue this necessary growth and keep pace with today's ever-advancing medical technology, Salinas Memorial Hospital Foundation, Inc., was created in 1979. The foundation was charged with the task of obtaining philanthropic contributions to help pay for hospital building expansion and acquisition of the latest diagnostic and therapeutic equipment. The foundation has a board of governors made up of 34 community leaders who, in 1987, contributed or encouraged friends to contribute more than $3 million in cash and pledges for hospital projects.

Though much of the hospital's growth from a local, 100-plus-bed hospital to a modern, 229-bed comprehensive medical center can be

seen through its acquisitions of the latest medical equipment, Salinas Valley Memorial also strives to combine high tech with high touch. The Orradre New Life Center, for example, provides personalized and comfortable surroundings for growing families in a growing community. In this facility, mother and baby have the advantage of modern hospital technology plus a warm, homey atmosphere that encourages family involvement and support.

And when mom needs a rest the Service League is standing by to help. The league's Cuddler Program provides volunteers to nurture and calm newborns during their hospital stay, giving new mothers a much-deserved break.

Cuddling babies is just one of many ways the Service League of volunteers works to support hospital ser-

Hospital employees can relax and enjoy lunch at the James R. Fassett, M.D., Plaza Courtyard, which features two local interest sculptures by Big Sur artist Emile Norman.

vices provided by Salinas Valley Memorial would simply not exist without these volunteers. Originally called The Women's League, the all-volunteer group has been an integral part of the hospital's operations since it was founded, contributing more than one million hours of service to both staff and patients since 1952.

Today more than 250 volunteers, including men, women, and teens, make up this auxiliary service arm. Volunteers staff the reception desks, guide visitors, and greet inpatients with daily mail and personal conveniences. They provide fresh flowers for the hospital's lobbies twice a week and even help out in areas such as surgery and the emergency room.

Through funds generated by its coffee and gift shops, the Service League has become a major financial contributor to many hospital projects. The league generates nearly $80,000 annually for equipment pur-

chases, expansion programs, in-house volunteer services, and community outreach projects that would not otherwise be available to the hospital. The group also provides a $7,500 scholarship each year to the Hartnell College nursing school to help with the current nursing shortage.

TeleCare and Tel-Med are two important new community outreach projects sponsored by the Service League. Through the TeleCare program, volunteers call anyone in the community who lives alone once a day to make certain they are alright. Tel-Med is the league's free medical information line, providing callers with more than 200 taped discourses on various medical disorders.

Outreach projects, such as TeleCare and Tel-Med, are just part of Salinas Valley Memorial's ongoing effort to promote good health for both hospital employees and the general public. The hospital's Health Promotion Program was started in 1976 in partnership with

the world-renowned Stanford Heart Disease Prevention Program. The effort focuses on encouraging good health habits and enhancing the quality and productivity of life through programs such as smoking cessation, nutritional education, and respiratory training, as well as community-wide fitness events, such as the annual Heart and Sole Race, co-sponsored by KSBW television.

Salinas Valley Memorial was also the first hospital in California to offer in-house, computerized, televised education. The hospital's Health Promotion Department provides special health video tapes for patients and employees on a convenient daily screening schedule.

Salinas Valley Memorial Hospital continues to strive to improve the quality of life for the growing Salinas Valley communities it serves through responsive, professional attention, the most advanced medical technology, and progressive health care programs. In an era of numerous and complex challenges, its commitment to consistently high professional standards reflects the commitment and strength of character of its founders and establishes Salinas Valley Memorial as a leader in the health care industry.

BUD OF CALIFORNIA

When Lester V. "Bud" Antle started his Salinas Valley produce packing and shipping company some 44 years ago, he was just one of many entrepreneurs starting out in the vegetable business—and lettuce was just one of many vegetable crops being grown in Monterey County.

But today lettuce is clearly the county's number-one crop, and Bud Antle, Inc., has become the largest grower/shipper of fresh vegetables in the world.

Antle is remembered as a pioneer who implemented dozens of innovations, in widespread use today, that significantly changed the fresh vegetable industry. Antle's company was the first local produce firm to field pack (packing produce in the field as it is picked) lettuce, celery, cauliflower, and broccoli. It was the first company to use vacuum cooling in the early 1950s. And it was the first to use corrugated cardboard cartons for packing vegetables. The company was also the first major grower/shipper opera-

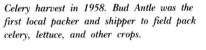
Celery harvest in 1958. Bud Antle was the first local packer and shipper to field pack celery, lettuce, and other crops.

tion in the Salinas Valley to recognize a union, signing a contract with the Teamsters in 1961.

Antle's company, which was first incorporated in 1961 as Bud Antle, Inc., was purchased in 1978 by Castle and Cooke, Inc., making it part of the Dole Food Group. In 1987 the firm's familiar brand name, "Bud of California," was changed to "Bud of California from Dole."

Bud, as the firm is commonly known, currently handles more than 25 different varieties of fresh veg-

etables. The company is twice the size of its nearest competitor, and it consistently controls 15 to 17 percent of the iceberg lettuce market.

Though it is best known as a lettuce producer, Bud is a recognized leader in other areas, too. Measured in both packages of product and in dollars, the firm also maintains the world's largest market share of cauliflower and celery.

Bud contracts with more than 50 independent growers, who farm 60,000 acres in nine strategic growing areas from Central California to northern Mexico and western Arizona. And the company employs as many as 3,500 people, making Bud the largest single employer in Monterey County.

Bud has developed and patented more cooling methods for fresh produce than the rest of the firms in the industry combined. The company now uses five different refrigeration techniques: icing, hydro-cooling, hydrovac cooling, pressure cooling, and vacuum cooling.

Most of Bud's Salinas Valley produce comes through the Marina

Hard at work to bring lettuce to American consumers, field workers for Bud Antle pack the 1966 harvest.

The 65,000-square-foot Marina Cooler Complex, the largest cooling and shipping facility in the world, is adjacent to Highway 1, south of Castroville.

Cooler Complex just off Highway 1. With 120 employees, the 65,000-square-foot facility is the largest refrigeration and shipping complex in the world. During peak season an average of 300 trucks per day are loaded from the cooling facility. The company ships approximately 40 million packages of produce annually.

To efficiently distribute its products, Bud employs a sophisticated computer system and satellite communications network that links the Bud sales offices in Salinas, Dallas, Chicago, Atlanta, and New York with the company's eight distribution centers and corporate headquarters.

But volume is not Bud's only goal. The company continues to improve product quality through its large research and development department on Old Stage Road in Salinas. There, plant pathologists and breeders utilize 55 experimental greenhouses to develop weather- and disease-resistant produce varieties to shorten growing time and provide a uniform, high-quality crop.

In the late 1960s the Bud organization recognized the need for a celery variety with resistance to seed stock formation, a problem during

winter production. Through the efforts of the company's first celery breeder, James Abe, the celery variety now known as Bud Special was developed. Bud Special is known throughout the industry for its smooth shanks and its resistance to both seed stock formation and diseases.

Bud is also working to develop a line of fresh, precut vegetables

known as "value-added" products. Located at Bud's Marina cooling facility, the company's Northern Salad Plant processes more than 175,000 pounds of fresh vegetables daily.

Bud's foodservice division supplies precut product, which carries a guaranteed 14-day shelf life, to foodservice markets in both bulk packaged and individual portions for direct sales to such major chains as Burger King and Taco Bell.

While most of Bud's produce is shipped throughout North America, significant quantities are also exported to Western Europe, Great Britain, Singapore, Korea, and the Pacific Basin. Lettuce and celery are two of the major exports, and 50 percent of the lettuce in Hong Kong carries the Bud label.

Since 1944 Bud has been a dynamic and innovative leader in the fresh produce industry. Today, as part of Castle and Cooke, the firm continues the tradition of industry leadership started by Bud Antle more than 40 years ago.

Giant letters spelling out the company name on the roof of Bud Antle's headquarters in 1958 foretell the firm's giant stature in the world produce industry.

LACEY AUTOMOTIVE PARTS COMPANY

Lacey Automotive Parts Company is the oldest continuously operating family-owned business in Monterey County. The firm has earned that distinction through the intelligent management and hard work of its many longtime employees and through a singular willingness to change with the times.

It's not surprising, therefore, to find that theme of change running through the history of the company beginning with its founding in 1867.

Salinas wasn't much of a town then, just a tiny farming community in need of a blacksmith. So when Joseph V. Lacey decided to set up shop in the Salinas Valley that year, he could have chosen to hang his sign practically anywhere from Natividad, near the Gabilan mountain range, to Hilltown, near the Salinas River. But instead the white-bearded blacksmith and wheelwright chose to establish his business on Monterey Street at Sausal (now Market) in downtown Salinas.

Lacey's enterprise was opened

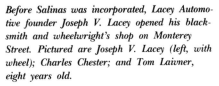

Before Salinas was incorporated, Lacey Automotive founder Joseph V. Lacey opened his blacksmith and wheelwright's shop on Monterey Street. Pictured are Joseph V. Lacey (left, with wheel); Charles Chester; and Tom Laivner, eight years old.

as a blacksmith shop and remained as such until 1911, when his son George finished expanding the company's services to accommodate the new horseless carriages that were beginning to file down Monterey Street with increasing regularity. He learned about the new technology as he went along, adapting his skills to service his customers' new modes of transportation. By 1928 the company had evolved from an

auto and truck repair garage into an automotive parts store.

Today Lacey Automotive Parts Company is one of the largest automotive parts distributors on the Central Coast. The firm has expanded throughout Monterey and San Benito counties by opening four additional stores in King City, Soledad, Seaside, and Hollister. Recently the company added a wholesale distribution center and an engine production facility.

And to keep up with the ever-increasing proliferation of auto parts, the company computerized its inventory in 1972. "Inventory control is vital to this business," says company president Robert Chapman. "There's been a parts explosion in this country. Where auto makers used to stay with the same engine for 10 years, now they sometimes change in the middle of the year. Stocking parts for all those engines

From its origins as a blacksmith shop, Lacey Automotive evolved into an auto parts store.

is a real challenge. Thank God for the computer."

Chapman's late wife, Diane, was Joseph V. Lacey's great-granddaughter. Their daughters, Lee Carroll and Leslie Taylor, and son William are great-great-grandchildren of the founder and all live in Salinas. William is manager of the Salinas store. Since the death of his first wife, Chapman has remarried. His second wife is Pat Tynan Chapman, whose family has operated Tynan Lumber Company in Salinas since 1912.

Chapman has taken an active interest in all aspects of his industry on both the state and national levels. He is a past president of the California Automotive Wholesalers Association and was its director for 10 years; he was director of the Automotive Service Industry Association for five years; and he is past president of the Pacific Automotive Show.

The company has also been rec-ognized three times by *Jobber Topics,* an industry trade publication, with articles on Lacey Automotive Parts published in 1948, 1976, and 1978.

The business has also been a pioneer in the area of employee benefits. In the early 1950s company managers offered workers one of the area's first health care packages, and in 1958 they introduced profit sharing.

"The quality of our employees is one of the reasons we've lasted so long," says Chapman. Nearly one-third of Lacey Automotive's 85 employees have been with the company for more than 10 years, approximately one-quarter for 20 years, and recently two Lacey employees retired after more than 50 years of service.

One of Lacey Automotive's biggest changes came in 1986, when the downtown Salinas urban-renewal project forced the com-

In 1986 Lacey Automotive moved from its original location in downtown Salinas to this 40,000-square-foot facility in the Ottone Business Park. Photo by Ron Starr, courtesy, Jerome Kasavan Associates, Inc.

pany to move. Construction of a new building, designed by longtime Salinas architect Jerome Kasavan, was completed in 1986. That same year, after 119 years of continuous operation in the same location, Lacey Automotive moved into its new home: a 40,000-square-foot facility set on two acres of the 55-acre Ottone Business Park located at John and Work streets in Salinas.

"We've made a lot of adjustments over the years," says Chapman, "both physically and philosophically. The product has changed, distribution patterns have changed, and the times have changed. No matter what business you're in, change is inevitable. Changing with the times is the way we've survived."

BANK OF SALINAS

The Bank of Salinas was founded in 1983 by a group of Salinas business leaders determined to establish something that they believed the community was missing—a truly local financial institution stressing customer service and a commitment to excellence.

Originally called the Farmers and Merchants Bank of Salinas, the new company opened for business on February 23 of its founding year. The name was shortened six months later to Bank of Salinas because the local entity was being confused with other banks in California bearing the Farmers and Merchants appellation.

The institution's founders chose the ground floor of a tall building on the corner of Main and Alisal streets for their new operation. That choice made it the third bank to occupy the structure, still the tallest in downtown Salinas, since it was built in 1929 for the Salinas National Bank. A story published that year in the *Salinas Index Journal,* forerunner of the *Salinas Californian,* stated that the building was ". . . the city's most

beautiful edifice, the most outstanding thing in the way of architecture in all the county."

The Bank of Salinas initially occupied only the building's first-floor mezzanine and four suites of offices on the second floor. By 1985, however, with more than double its original staff, the company had moved into additional second-floor offices and occupied the entire third floor as well.

The bank's commitment to the kind of friendly, personal service that has been all but lost in many financial institutions, as well as its intimate knowledge of business and banking in the Salinas Valley, continued to fuel its growth. By the end of the second quarter of 1988 the company's assets exceeded $112 million.

In its five years of operation the institution has made more than 10,000 loans to Salinas Valley businesses and individuals, and today services more than 7,000 accounts. Currently, approximately 830 shareholders own a total of 1.053 million shares of Bank of Salinas stock.

As the bank's assets have grown, so has its community involvement. In 1985 the Bank of Salinas

joined the City of Salinas and the Salinas Area Chamber of Commerce in sponsoring the Salinas Business Excellence Awards. This annual event, the only one of its kind in the area, continues to recognize companies whose outstanding efforts have helped the entire region to prosper. The bank has also strongly encouraged downtown redevelopment and will play an active role in the organization and development of the Steinbeck Center.

Customer service and convenience has been at the heart of the Bank of Salinas management philosophy from its inception, so it's

The Bank of Salinas building at 301 Main Street (tall structure at right) was erected in 1929 for the Salinas National Bank.

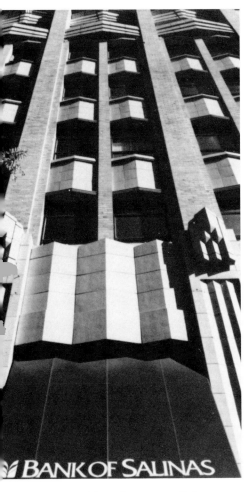

BANK OF SALINAS

The Bank of Salinas was founded by community business leaders seeking to establish a locally owned and operated financial institution.

Green, president of Green's Camera Shop; Duncan L. McCarter, Salinas pharmacist and president of Care Pharmacies, Inc.; Robert L. Meyer, president of Meyer Tomatoes, Inc.; Robert M. Mraule, D.D.S., M.D., a Salinas oral surgeon; and Harry D. Wardwell, Jr., manager of Wardwell's Magnavox.

In 1984 the bank activated yet another innovation in the form of the Bank of Salinas Advisory Board. The board is comprised of a group of 42 individuals whose business and community contacts and re-

not surprising that one of the company's more innovative programs focuses on that very idea. The Trip Saver Service provides bank customers with a bonded service representative to pick up deposits at their offices and places of business.

Guiding the Bank of Salinas is a board of directors drawn from among the community's most successful and respected leaders in business and the professions. Nick Ventimiglia, president and director on the board, is a longtime Salinas resident with more than 23 years in banking. Other board members include Andrew E. Ausonio, president of Ausonio Construction, Inc.; C. Edward Boutonnet, general manager of Sea-Mist Farms and Boutonnet Farms, Inc.; Roger G. Emanuel, president of Russell-Roger, Inc.; Richard C.

lationships provide the bank with a variety of opinions and ideas.

The Bank of Salinas has been building a solid financial foundation within the community since 1983 by increasing its specialized services and reinvesting in local projects. The confidence and credibility of the company is reflected in the decisions of local businesses, individuals, and public agencies, such as the City of Salinas and the Salinas Union High School District, to choose this local bank.

The founders of the Bank of Sa-

Top: To show its appreciation for its customers, the Bank of Salinas frequently hosts festive receptions in the lobby.

Above: A special free Artichoke Day has been included among the bank's many areas of community involvement.

linas sought to create a strong, stable, locally owned, managed, and involved financial institution—and they succeeded. The concepts upon which the bank was founded have proven to be sound, and they will continue to guide the Bank of Salinas for many years to come.

THE LANTIS CORPORATION

When engineer Bing Lantis purchased the Cochran Western Corporation in 1983, the troubled company was losing money, customers, and prestige. But within a few months of its purchase, the firm's bleeding had stopped, and the new Lantis Corporation was on its way to becoming the largest airline ground support equipment manufacturer in the world.

In fact the original enterprise, called Cochran Equipment Company after its founder, Joseph Cochran, a chemical engineer and M.I.T. graduate, did not specialize at all. From early egg-candling equipment to prototypes of some of the first lettuce field-wide track trucks, Cochran Equipment had designed and fabricated a variety of machinery during the early 1950s.

But by 1957 Cochran had begun building ground support equipment for United Airlines. At that time few U.S. manufacturers were producing such specialized machinery, so demand was high and Cochran's company thrived. Later he

Used by airline and overnight freight companies worldwide, Lantis' TLC 818 Container/Pallet Loader is designed to handle large loading jobs.

moved his operation from the corner of Monterey and Pajaro streets in Salinas into a new, larger plant located at the Salinas Airport.

Cochran sold his operation in 1968 to Western Gear, which formed a new company called Cochran Western. Though Cochran's firm had been a leader within its narrow field of competitors, the new enterprise failed to prosper under its new management. Competitors developed new products while Cochran Western's equipment became outdated and unreliable. The operation lost customers, dwindled in size, and eventually the ailing manufacturer's owners began looking for a buyer.

The buyer they found was Bing Lantis, who had been an engineer and operations manager for Cochran and then Western Gear for more than 13 years. Though

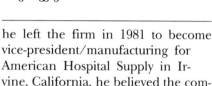

Lantis' TLC 610 Electric Mobile Belt Loader is widely used by passenger airlines for handling baggage.

he left the firm in 1981 to become vice-president/manufacturing for American Hospital Supply in Irvine, California, he believed the company was a viable operation that was being mismanaged. Lantis made his former employers an offer, and two weeks later The Lantis Corporation was off and running.

Lantis quickly established a renewed commitment to product improvement and stopped the debilitating exodus of customers that had diminished the company during the years. Within its second month under new management, the manufacturer recorded its first profits in years. By the end of its first 18 months as The Lantis Corporation, the firm nearly tripled its work force, and sales were passing the monthly million-dollar mark.

By 1988 orders for The Lantis Corporation's equipment exceeded the Salinas plant's capacity, necessitating the firm to open another plant in Hernando, Mississippi, to produce the company's freight-sensitive machinery.

The Lantis Corporation also continues its long-standing support of the Carriage Company, a nonprofit employer of the handicapped founded by Cochran Western Corporation.

In just a few short years The Lantis Corporation is once again the largest supplier of aircraft unit loading equipment in the world.

FRESH WESTERN MARKETING, INC.

Tom Church had never planned to go into business for himself; but when he and his partners decided to set up Fresh Western Marketing, Inc., he was confident that the new company would make an impact. He just didn't expect it to happen so quickly.

Church, who is president and chief executive officer of Fresh Western, has more than 25 years' experience in the produce business. For 12 of those years he worked for Bruce Church, Inc. (BCI), as the firm's sales manager until the early part of 1981, when he became disenchanted with his work and resigned.

The moment Church resigned, however, he knew he would start his own business. And he knew it would be a produce company. So, after a much-needed two-week vacation, Church began making plans for his enterprise.

It wasn't long before Church's good friends, Steve Wolfe and Noel Carr, heard about his project and offered to join him. Wolfe had been in charge of pre-cut lettuce operations at BCI, and Carr was in charge of harvesting operations. Church accepted their offer

Trucks await loading at Fresh Western's latest facility, built in 1987.

Several of the 100 produce items that Fresh Western markets weekly.

gratefully.

About two weeks after the three partners had set up shop, they were joined by another friend and BCI alumnus, Mike Domingos. Domingos had worked in sales for BCI for 10 years, and his father was a grower for the company.

One month into the project, Clem Richardson, who had taken Church's place as BCI's sales manager, left his job and joined his friends at Fresh Western. Later Jim Storm and Steve Church also teamed up with Fresh Western.

Initially the organization formed by these five men acted as a produce broker and distributor. But Fresh Western Marketing experienced rapid growth in its first five years of operation as it quickly expanded its services, becoming a sales agent, a harvester, and even adding a cooling facility. Today Fresh Western continues to be one of the produce industry's fastest-expanding full-service grower/shippers.

Unlike most of its competitors, who have historically concentrated on one or two produce items, Fresh Western sells more than 100 different produce items, creating a one-stop shopping service for food-service distributors and produce retailers.

Fresh Western has also been an innovator in establishing a network of distributors for its products. Through this network Fresh Western can provide its River Ranch brand products to customers nationwide.

To cope with the ever-changing demands of consumers, Fresh Western has been a leader in developing pre-cut and "value-added" products. To keep pace with changes in the produce markets, the firm has expanded its operations to include exports to the Pacific Rim, Western Europe, and the Far West, as well as imports from Mexico, Chile, and Caribbean countries.

In a very short time Fresh Western Marketing, Inc., has established itself as a market leader in one of California's most competitive industries. Today the company is one of that industry's most effective marketing links between grower and customer.

SALINAS VALLEY WAX PAPER COMPANY

Neither of the two founders of the Salinas Valley Wax Paper Company had much knowledge of the paper business when they first set out to establish a bread wrap operation in the mid-1920s. But the firm they created has survived a corporate evolution that spans three generations.

The company founders, Charles E. Goetz and T.G. Emmons, met while working in the Arizona mining industry. Although they shared an interest in the mining business, they were two very different men.

Charlie Goetz, former grocery boy from Buffalo, New York, had barely made it through the eighth grade. But he had a quick and imaginative mind, which he applied throughout his life to an array of entrepreneurial schemes. In 1925 he was operating a general store in Benson, Arizona.

But Goetz' store was losing money and he wanted to get into another line of business. He had the idea of starting a wax paper company to produce the new paper bread wrappers that were becoming popular.

Goetz was an idea man, a promoter. He knew he could not hold

Charlie Goetz stands before one of his many inventions—a vacuum cooling tube for fresh produce use.

up to the technical end of such an operation and needed a partner who could make his ideas work.

So Goetz took his idea to Guy Emmons, who had studied mining engineering at the University of Arizona at Tucson and had come to Benson to pursue a career in that industry. But mining had begun its decline, and Emmons was about to open an auto repair garage when Goetz convinced him to invest $500 and join in the wax paper enterprise.

Goetz and Emmons set up their first wax paper operation in Benson in 1926. Their biggest customer turned out to be a local dynamite manufacturer, the Apache Powder Company, which used the paper to line its powder cases. The bread wrap idea had failed because of production and marketing problems. If the firm was going to survive it was going to need more customers. So Goetz traveled to Yuma to sell waxed crate liners to the lettuce shippers there.

That was when he met Bruce Church. Goetz was having lunch in a Yuma hotel restaurant one day during his trip when a bellboy paged Church. Goetz asked his luncheon companions who Church was, and they told him he was an important lettuce shipper from Salinas, California.

As soon as Church hung up the phone he found himself facing the engaging Goetz. The two men talked at length about the lettuce business in the Salinas Valley. When Church complained that he was paying too much for crate liners and suggested that the area could use a manufacturer, Goetz knew he had found the market he was looking for. He promptly sent a telegram to Benson and caught the first train to California.

The enterprise's first Salinas operation opened in 1928 in a portion of a Spreckels Sugar Company warehouse. Emmons moved to Salinas at that time to run the new operation, while Goetz returned to Benson. Emmons operated the plant in Spreckels for nine years and, despite the onset of the Great Depression, the company grew—so much that in 1937 the operation was moved to a new, 13,000-square-foot facility on Highway 101, now Abbott Street, just outside Salinas.

For the next 17 years the firm continued to grow, becoming an important supplier of waxed paper products for the produce industry. The Benson plant was eventually closed, and Goetz started an ice company and packing shed operation near Phoenix. Management of the wax paper operation was left to Emmons.

At the start of World War II, all but three of the company's employees joined the armed forces. During that time Emmons, his foreman, and Emmons' young son-in-law, Gaylord H. Nelson, worked long hours with limited qualified help, six days per week, producing waterproof laminated kraft paper for the war effort.

In the early 1950s vacuum cooling technology revolutionized Salinas Valley fresh produce shipping operations. With the new process, corrugated cartons were used, and lettuce packers needed very little ice to ship their produce, and they did not require wooden crates or wax paper liners.

Ironically, the man who first encouraged Goetz and Emmons to bring their business to Salinas was the one who nearly closed it down. Bruce Church was the principal figure in founding Growers Container Corporation, which manufactured the new fresh produce corrugated containers. Emmons and Goetz could not compete in that field.

Salinas Valley Wax Paper did cope, however, with this nearly devastating change by diversifying its product line. Limited production of certain liner papers for row crops that were still crated, such as celery and green onions, continued as before. But the line of laminated asphalt paper was increased to include laminated foil, flashing

paper, and other special grades for the building industry. The company survived and even prospered with added waxed and other lines.

In 1956 Emmons retired from active management of the Salinas Valley Wax Paper Company, and Gay Nelson became a limited partner. Emmons died two years later in Sedona, Arizona, and Mrs. Emmons sold her interest in the operation to the Nelson family.

Charlie Goetz sold his interest in the company to the Nelsons in 1969, but continued to actively pursue a variety of enterprises until his death at age 93.

In 1970 Charles Emmons Nelson joined the firm as general manager, making the Salinas Valley Wax Paper Company a third-generation family operation.

Gay and Charles Nelson have continued to diversify their firm's product line and successfully adapt to

an ever-changing marketplace. In 1974 they added a four-color printing press to broaden their production capabilities. They later introduced waxed and shredded florist tissues, printed tissue, wine bottle wraps, oiled meat wraps, and a broad range of specialty paper items. Recent additions to sheet cutters, laminating, and roll-rewinding equipment have expanded size of product line and maximized versatility, service, and quality.

By focusing on innovation, hard work, and integrity at all levels of operation, the Salinas Valley Wax Paper Company has weathered a storm of change with its competent administrative and production force, and will keep going strong for another 60 years.

The first Salinas Valley Wax Paper Company operation was in a warehouse at the Spreckels Sugar Company plant near Salinas.

GOLDEN WEST RESTAURANTS

Herb Rothstein opened his first Golden West Pancakes operation in Redwood City, California, in 1962. But it wasn't the first restaurant he had opened, and it wouldn't be the last.

Rothstein came to California from a small town in Minnesota in 1940 to live with his brother, Leonard, in Watsonville. At that time he attended Salinas Junior College (Hartnell College) during the day and washed dishes in the Pet Creamery restaurant at night. Rothstein was a hard worker and a natural organizer, and before the year was done, he had worked his way up to manager.

In 1941 Rothstein left his job and joined the United States Navy. When he left the service he went to Alaska to homestead 200 acres. But his stay in the North wasn't a long one. "The saying up there was, 'When the snow piles six feet on a fence post, it's time to leave Alaska,'" says Rothstein. "Well it didn't

The second Golden West Pancake House opened in Salinas in June 1966.

take the damned snow long to bury all the fence posts I could see and I got the heck out of there."

Rothstein returned to California and settled in Santa Cruz where he worked as a cook at Bosley's Drive-In, and later at the Rio Del Mar Hotel. Eventually he took a job at the Lucky Store Restaurant in the Valley Center in Salinas. The sign in the window read "Waitress Wanted," but he applied for the job anyway. After doing a real selling job, he won the position and three weeks later was the restaurant's new manager.

In 1953 Rothstein finally decided to try the business that he seemed to have such a flair for on his own. Along with his brother, Harley, he opened the Pine Drive-In Restaurant in Seaside. Herb's wife, Fran, helped the

brothers operate their new enterprise, which seated 40 people inside and accommodated 25 cars outside. The new drive-in's menu was designed by Hank Ketchum, creator of the "Dennis the Menace" comic strip. Ketchum didn't charge Rothstein for the design, but insisted on being invited to the opening party.

With the success of the Pine Drive-In, Rothstein decided to open another restaurant, this time in Salinas. The Sherwood Gardens drive-in restaurant was built in 1956 on North Main Street across from the rodeo grounds. From day one, the new operation was a gold mine. Rothstein recalls opening the doors of his new restaurant on a Thursday morning and being so busy that he was forced to close them on Friday evening because he had sold all the food. That night he woke up all his purveyors so that he could buy supplies for the next morning.

The Sherwood, which 20 years later became the Blue Boar Inn, was for years the only restaurant on the north side of town. It seated 80 people inside and served 40 outside. Car hops wore Robin Hood uniforms, and a 300-foot mural of Sherwood Forest, painted by local artist Russell Swan, adorned the wall behind the back counter.

In 1960 Rothstein formed a part-

Herb Rothstein receives a dime from Eleanor Roosevelt during his 1964 Miles of Dimes campaign for the March of Dimes.

nership with A.C. Bingham, and together they opened the Old Fashioned Pancake House on the corner of Laurel Drive and North Main Street. He eventually bought out his partner and turned the restaurant into Golden West Pancake House.

But Rothstein's first Golden West Pancakes operation wasn't opened until 1962. "It was in Redwood City," says Rothstein, "and I got that restaurant this way: A couple I knew went up there and bought a restaurant and remodeled it. One night the wife called me and said, 'My husband is going to have a heart attack. You better get up here and take this restaurant.' I said, 'How am I going to do that?' She said, 'If you'll just take it over you can have it.' Well, I was never given a better deal than that so I took it. I hadn't even seen it and had no idea what it looked like, but we took everybody up there and changed it almost overnight. It was crazy, but sometimes things happen like that."

At that time pancake houses were springing up nationwide. They were very popular with young parents looking for an inexpensive way to take their children out to eat. Rothstein's early operations offered an extensive menu of pancakes, from buttermilk and blueberry to chocolate chip, and at each table was a selection of eight different syrups.

By the early 1970s the pancake craze was beginning to wane, and in 1975 Rothstein changed the name of his operations to Golden West Restaurants and expanded his menu to include lunch and dinner entrees. But the breakfast menu is still the most popular at Golden West, and it's offered 24 hours per day.

Rothstein's three sons grew up working in the family business and

are now an integral part of the operation. Rodney Rothstein, now president of Golden West Restaurants, recalls that his father didn't pay them well in the old days. "Back then he'd tell mom to bring us down to the restaurant for dinner," says Rodney. "After we finished eating we'd be handed an apron and find ourselves working for a couple of hours. Then we'd hold out our hands and Dad would say, 'What's that for? You got to eat didn't you?"

Gary Rothstein, executive vice-president of Golden West, says that

The Rothsteins (from left): Steve Rothstein, vice-president and manager of Golden West Supply Company; Herb Rothstein (seated), chairman of the board and co-founder of the first Golden West Pancake House; Gary Rothstein, general manager of Golden West Supply Company and executive vice-president of Golden West Restaurants; and Rodney Rothstein, president and chief executive officer of Golden West Restaurants.

when he and his brothers were children, they were holy terrors when they came into the restaurant. "They liked to keep us in the car," he says.

Steve Rothstein remembers standing on milk crates when he was three years old while the dishwasher let him help scrub pans.

Steve is vice-president and manager of Golden West Supply Company, which opened in 1978, originally to serve its own restaurants. But the demand from other area restaurants soon grew, and today Golden West Supply serves more than 200 other operations in the tri-

county area.

The Rothstein family today operates 19 Golden West Restaurants (there are no franchises) throughout Northern California and Nevada. From a small diner with eight employees it has grown to an operation employing more than 600 people. In 1980 Golden West received a national Award of Merit in the Golden Pyramid Competition for its Golden Years Club promotion for senior citizens. In 1982 the company was given the Achievement Award from *Restaurant Hospitality Magazine* as one of the top 500

commercial food operations in the United States.

"It's been a lot of work," says Herb Rothstein of his 35 years in the restaurant business. "A *lot* of work. But mostly, it's been a lot of fun."

THE NUNES COMPANY, INC.

Growing and shipping produce is a risky business. Often the vegetables are sold for less than the cost of growing them, and a company can fall by the wayside in a single down market. But to Tom and Bob Nunes, those risks are outweighed by the opportunities. Finding those opportunities has made Nunes Company, Inc., a pioneer in the produce industry.

But pioneering is nothing new to the Nunes brothers; it is a tradition that was established by their father, Tom Nunes, Sr., who immigrated to America from the Azores

Robert Nunes (right) and Clark Drury in the Growers Exchange sales office. Photo circa 1958

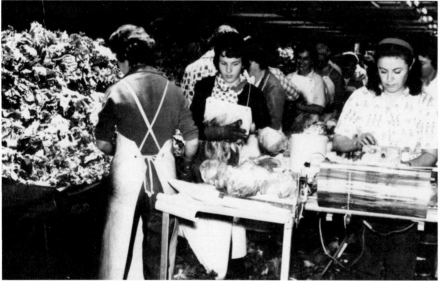

An early film-wrap operation at Growers Exchange. Photo circa 1960

islands near Portugal in 1907. Nunes later moved to the Salinas Valley and took up farming in the early 1930s.

Nunes eventually became a large and successful grower. He was one of the founders of the Salinas Marketing Cooperative and the Salinas Lettuce Farmers Cooperative, which are two local vegetable shipping organizations owned by the growers that supply them. His sons, Tom and Bob, worked with him on the ranches while they were growing up.

Both Tom and Bob Nunes went to local Salinas schools and

later attended Stanford University, where they studied economics. After finishing college, young Tom began farming with his father under the partnership of T. Nunes and Son. But in 1955 he, along with Clark Drury, Hal Moller, Bill Brown, and Bob Gargiulo, founded Growers Exchange, Inc. The new enterprise, primarily a grower/shipper of lettuce, began with 400 acres that Tom and his partners harvested and shipped.

After his college graduation a

few years later, Bob spent six years in the produce industry. He first worked as a county inspector, then as a bookkeeper for Pacific Packing Company, and finally as a salesman for the Kavanagh Distributing Company.

Bob finally joined his brother, Tom, at Growers Exchange in 1959. During the next seven years the organization grew rapidly, becoming one of the West's leading lettuce grower/shippers.

Tom and Bob Nunes continued with Growers Exchange until 1966, when they left the company to form Nunes Brothers of California, with 5,000 acres of produce in the Salinas and Imperial valleys. They grew and shipped lettuce, cauliflower, and celery from the Salinas area, and lettuce and cantaloupes from the Imperial Valley. The following year they expanded their operation into Arizona, and by the end of 1968 they were growing and shipping 7,000 crop acres annually.

During the new company's first growing season, the Nunes brothers implemented a marketing idea that was previously unheard of in

After an early and brief retirement, Bob (left) and Tom Nunes founded the Nunes Company, which has increased its operation from 1,200 acres of lettuce and cauliflower in 1976 to 10,000 acres today.

the produce industry. They offered consumers a premium with the purchase of a head of lettuce: a discount on the price of a popular seasoned salt.

They were able to make use of this important new marketing tool because of another industry innovation: prepackaged produce. Always looking for new and better ways to do the job, the Nunes brothers were among the first to film-wrap lettuce. The idea was very successful and brought their firm to the attention of the United Fruit Sales Corporation.

Tom and Bob sold their operation to United Fruit, the company famous for Chiquita-brand bananas, in 1968. The corporation purchased several other area produce companies about that time and eventually formed Inter Harvest, later called Sun Harvest, which became the largest vegetable operation in the country.

Tom and Bob stayed on as managers of the new operation until August 1970, when they did something that stunned the produce industry contemporaries—they re-

tired. Tom was 41 and Bob was 39 years of age.

When the brothers left the firm, they were required to stay out of the growing and shipping of vegetables for at least five years. During that time they traveled, tried new things, and spent time with their families—time they just didn't have during the years they were building their business.

By 1976 both men had become bored with retirement and began to look to the produce business again. They thought there might be a place for a premium-type pack-

age in the lettuce industry. Their agreement with United Fruit had expired the year before, and they decided it was time to get back to work. They called their new firm The Nunes Company, Inc.

Just six years earlier Tom and Bob had co-managed the largest vegetable operation in the United States. But when they returned from their mid-life retirement, it was as two employees. Bob did the selling, Tom did the growing, and two of their former employees, Trini Gomez and Jess Gomez (not related), who had stayed with Inter Har-

vest until the Nunes brothers returned to the business, handled the harvesting.

The Nunes Company began operating with 1,200 crop acres. Today, with millions of dollars worth of equipment and plants in Salinas and in Yuma, Arizona, the fully integrated grower/shipper handles more than 10,000 crop acres of lettuce and cauliflower annually.

The third generation of the Nunes family is firmly in place in the new venture as well. Bob's son, Bob Nunes, Jr., works in quality control and labor; Tom's eldest

Grower Exchange's first field packing machine in operation in the early 1960s.

son, Tom Nunes, Jr., works in sales; and Tom's two younger sons, David and Jim, work in the company's growing operations.

The Nunes Company continues the Nunes family tradition of produce industry pioneering with innovative marketing strategies that have brought its premium labels, Foxy and Tubby, widespread consumer recognition. Turning risks into opportunities has made The Nunes Company, Inc., an industry leader.

FRESH INTERNATIONAL

When Bruce Church embarked on his first produce venture he had only one partner and a solitary field of lettuce. But that single, small enterprise would one day grow into four of the produce industry's most respected companies. Today Fresh International and its subsidiaries, Bruce Church, Inc., BC Systems, FreshCo, and Trans-FRESH, continue a tradition of excellence and innovation that began more than 60 years ago.

Church's first venture into the produce business was a partnership formed in 1926 with Whitney Knowlton. With $3,000 start-up capital provided by Knowlton, the two bought a field of lettuce ready for harvest. As Church had predicted, the venture was a great success—so successful, in fact, that Knowlton's loan to the partnership was repaid in just two weeks, and the pair split a fine profit.

Church never forgot that it took borrowed money to launch his first enterprise, and throughout his life he helped many people get started in the produce busi-

Bruce Church, founder (1900-1958).

ness. "We've always had a policy of helping young people," Church said in a story published in the *Carmel Spectator/Journal* in 1956. "I like to see young people get ahead. Many of them have ambition and the ability to work, but haven't any cash. So we'll sometimes step in and give them a push."

With such a philosophy it's not surprising that during his career Church attracted a great many business partners. In 1937 he formed a partnership with Ken Nutting, Gene Harden, and Russell Merrill—three other important names in the produce business—and founded Growers Ice and Development Company to provide his burgeoning industry with ice-packing services it needed to ship fresh vegetables. In 1954 Church joined with Lester V. "Bud" Antle, another prominent figure in agriculture, to buy the plants and patents of The Vacuum Cooling Company and make this modern cooling process available to local produce shippers. That same year, with a group of local produce shippers, he founded Growers Container Company to manufacture locally the corrugated containers used for vacuum-cooled products.

Since Church's death in 1958 there have been many changes in his company. During the early days, and continuing into the 1960s, the firm had been involved in many different types of agriculture, from cattle feeding and cotton growing operations to strawberry and citrus production. By 1975, about the time Fresh International was formed as a holding company for all Bruce Church interests, the organization had liquidated its involvement in many of these areas and began to focus on fresh vegetables.

Today Bruce Church, Inc. (BCI), grows iceberg lettuce, broccoli, cauliflower, and red leaf and green leaf lettuce. The company is

As agricultural pioneers who founded Growers Ice and Development Company, these four men helped to make the Salinas Valley the nation's Salad Bowl. From left are Russell Merrill, Bruce Church, Ken Nutting, and Gene Harden.

fully integrated—growing, harvesting, and cooling much of the produce it markets. With five areas of production—Salinas, Santa Maria, and the San Joaquin Valley in California, and Yuma and Parker in Arizona—the firm moves virtually the same volume of produce each week of the year.

BCI's deep-rooted tradition of innovation has led it to develop

many firsts that have had a lasting effect on the entire produce industry.

BCI developed farm equipment and modernized techniques for planting and fertilizing that were eventually adopted by the rest of the industry. The company was the first grower to ship 100 percent of its product on pallets or floor racks to enhance refrigeration in transit. And

BCI led the industry in the development and application of pesticide safety procedures and controls that have been used as a model by legislatures in California and Arizona.

BCI was the first produce company in the Salinas Valley to use sprinkler irrigation on lettuce crops. This approach resulted in considerable water conservation, improved uniformity, and increased yields.

Always an important developer of lettuce varieties, BCI was instrumental in cultivating hardier plants for varying desert conditions. With these developments the entire industry was able to move production of iceberg lettuce into Yuma, Arizona, and the Imperial Valley of California during the winter months. BCI's new focus on fresh produce

BCI harvest operations in the mid-1950s (below), and in 1988 (left).

TECTROL Atmosphere is injected into a sealed load of strawberries.

items in general, and lettuce in particular, helped to generate a greater drive to develop new and improved varieties of seed. Through 1987 many of these new developments were offered commercially through another Fresh International company, Quali-sel. Though Quali-sel ceased operations in 1987, BCI continues its seed research and development efforts.

Regardless of the crop being grown, BCI has always sought out the finest-possible farmland and employed the most scientific land development techniques to assure maximum production of quality crops. A good example of this is the company's 6,400-acre Parker Ranch development.

The Parker Ranch project involved the conversion of thousands of acres of mesquite-patched, unimproved Colorado River bottom land into one of the finest irrigated row

crop farms in the world. Development required four years and included the relocation of more than 6 million cubic yards of earth to form 160 separate 40-acre irrigated plots with uniform soil structure. In addition, it involved the laying in excess of 40 miles of underground concrete irrigation pipe.

Developing new ideas is nothing new at Fresh International. In 1964 Whirlpool Corporation and Bruce Church initiated a joint research program to commercialize TECTROL Atmosphere for use in transportation. Whirlpool Corporation was deeply involved in life support technology being used in the U.S. space program. Also, it was the leading supplier of controlled atmosphere systems to apple and pear growers worldwide. The technology for the CA system came from the Servel gas refrigerator patents that were owned by Whirlpool. The firm was looking for new ways to preserve fresh foods with this technology and indeed found that by altering gas atmosphere, the respiration rate of fresh produce could be slowed down, preserving the produce for longer periods of time.

Whirlpool wanted to identify its commercial uses and needed BCI's help to do it. After two years of cooperative efforts on a research and development basis, TransFRESH was formed in 1966 as a joint-venture company for the purpose of manufacturing and marketing TECTROL Atmosphere systems.

TECTROL Atmosphere is not an additive or preservative. It is a gas mixture that is used to supplement refrigeration, slowing the rate at which chilled perishables

At TransFRESH, pallets of strawberries are bagged and sealed prior to the application of TECTROL, an atmospheric agent that ensures the freshness of the fruit during shipping.

FreshCo lettuce is cored and inspected prior to packaging.

breathe. In the breathing process, vegetables consume their internal sugar and give off water and carbon dioxide gas. It is this breathing process, coupled with bacterial growth, that leads to loss of freshness and breakdown. TECTROL slows the breathing rate, retards the bacterial growth rate, and extends the life of fresh cut vegetables. In 1976 Fresh International acquired Whirlpool's interest in TransFRESH. Today TransFRESH Corporation is an international leader in research, development, and application of modified and controlled atmosphere processes for the fresh food industry, whether it be in transportation or storage.

TransFRESH has consistently been a leader in developing new applications for gas atmospheres for extending the useful life of chilled perishables. Palletized products, such as strawberries, were put into pallet bags with injected modified atmosphere very successfully since the late 1960s. Another development by TransFRESH was learning how to tighten railcars, piggyback vans, and ocean containers satisfactorily so that they would contain TECTROL Atmosphere.

TransFRESH's development of

modified atmosphere technology for cut vegetable packaging soon led Fresh International to return to a product line from its past. In the early 1960s BCI had tried producing pre-cut vegetables for the food-service industry—an idea that was ahead of its time—but discontinued the operation because of the short shelf life of the products.

With the evolving modified atmosphere technology developed by TransFRESH, the company re-entered the prepared fresh vegetable market. In 1979 a new firm, FreshCo, Incorporated, was founded to handle the growing demand for precut vegetables.

FreshCo specializes in providing prepared produce for the food-service industry. The firm operates in close proximity to Fresh International's BC Systems cooling plants, from where it cuts, washes, packages, and distributes its products nationwide.

FreshCo was the first company to use the new modified atmosphere technology developed by Trans-

Packages of pre-cut salad mix for the food-service industry are injected with modified atmosphere and sealed at FreshCo.

FRESH in packaging fresh cut vegetables. The firm was also the first to utilize new types of polyethylene materials to control the transmission rates of carbon dioxide and oxygen gas molecules to prolong produce shelf life.

In addition to pre-cut lettuce, FreshCo provides a full line of prepared fresh vegetable products. This line includes cleaned and cored head lettuce, trimmed head lettuce, broccoli florets, cauliflower florets, carrot sticks, shredded carrots, and cabbage, celery, and onion products.

FreshCo continues to take a progressive approach to product research and development. The firm is currently conducting experiments in microwaveable packages and beginning to market prepared vegetables to supermarkets.

Throughout the activities of all these Fresh International companies there runs the recurring theme of innovation, quality, value, and just plain "fresh." It's a theme that resembles a favorite slogan of the late Bruce Church himself: "Our goal is this: To bring our customers the finest quality lettuce we, or anyone else, can possibly produce."

JIM BARDIN RANCH

The cattle business has changed since Jim Bardin's grandfather first traveled to the Salinas Valley more than 100 years ago. But at the Bardin Ranch one thing hasn't changed: It's still a family business. And the history of this particular business is the history of a family.

James Bardin, of Wayne County, North Carolina, was born in 1810 and was the first member of his family to travel to the Salinas Valley. He left his home in 1830 at the age of 20 to seek his fortune in Alabama, later going farther west to Tippah County, Mississippi, where he and his wife, Lucinda Walker, settled for the next 25 years to raise a family.

By 1855 James became restless and left his family in search of farmland in the promising West, arriving in Yreka, California, on August 11 of that year. He soon moved on to Sacramento, then San Francisco, and eventually found his way to the Salinas Valley.

James bought the farmland he had set out to find in the Salinas Valley and returned to Mississippi to gather his family. In March 1856, after the family crossed the Isthmus of Panama, the steamer *Cortez* arrived in San Francisco Bay carrying James, Lucinda, and their six children to their new home in the West.

One of the first orders of business for the newcomers was to register a cattle brand. A brand was then, and is today, of critical importance to anyone in the beef cattle business; it is a certificate of ownership that protects a rancher's livelihood. James registered his brand, which consisted of the capital letters "J" and "B" joined at the center and burned into the animal's left hip, in 1860. The Bardins still pay an annual registration fee to keep the brand.

James and Lucinda soon

settled into their new home and produced four more children for a total of 10. Bardin, who would not allow anyone to photograph him, died in 1888.

Among Bardin's four California-born children was James II, who was born near Salinas in 1856. This second James became a successful Salinas Valley farmer and cattleman. Along with his brother, Henry, he bought 17,000 acres of land east of Salinas from Jesse D. Carr. This land was part of the

James Bardin II (pictured) is remembered by his son Jim as being an honest, hardworking man who was "tough but fair." Photo circa 1906

Cienega del Gabilan Rancho, which originally consisted of 11 square leagues (nearly 50,000 acres) and was owned by Antonio Chavez. Chavez claimed that the land was part of an 1843 grant from then-governor of Mexico Michel-torena.

During the late 1800s the younger James Bardin II became the principal sugar beet grower for Claus Spreckels. His beet production prompted the construction, in 1898, of the world's largest sugar beet processing factory in what is

now Spreckels, California.

Along with his sugar beets Bardin was known for his crops of Burbank potatoes and was at one time considered the industry's "Potato King." He also raised cattle and helped pioneer the use of beet by-products in feeding them.

In 1906 James Bardin II married Danish-born Lena Petersen, the daughter of a blacksmith. The entire Petersen family, including 11 children, would eventually emigrate to California and settle in the Salinas Valley.

That same year James built a hospital for the City of Salinas on the corner of John and South Main streets, where Great Western Bank currently stands. He disliked the name James so he called it the Jim Bardin Hospital. His two children, Jim G. and Marie, were born there.

Jim G. Bardin worked with his father farming and tending cattle from the time he was a youngster until he was old enough to run the ranch himself. He remembers the elder James as an honest, hardworking man who was tough but fair and had a truly western philosophy: "Live each day so you can look every damned man in the eye and tell him to go to hell."

"If you're honest you can do that," says Bardin. "If you're a crook, you can't." James Bardin II died in 1932.

Jim G. Bardin recalls driving his father's herds down South Main Street in Salinas during the fall to a field at the south end of town to feed the cattle on beet tops. "Of course, in those days," recalls Bardin, "when we shipped cattle from here, we had to take them down to the railroad. And the railroad corrals were across the tracks from the present depot. We'd take them down to Front Street, then we'd go out to where

Young Jim Bardin rides the range with his father. Photo circa 1922

the PG&E plant is, then across North Main Street and back to the railroad corrals.

"It sure would be something to run cattle up and down Main Street now, wouldn't it?"

Jim attended school in Salinas and later went on to graduate from Stanford University in 1930. Upon the death of his father in 1932, he took over management of the Bardin ranches, both farming and beef cattle operations. James Bardin II and his brother Henry had divided their property in 1920, so the ranch Jim managed consisted of 8,000 acres east of Salinas, extend-

After 65 years of riding the range, Jim Bardin still sits tall in the saddle.

ing from Old Stage Road to Fremont Peak. He also farmed 1,000 acres in the Alisal area.

Bardin has seen a lot of changes in his ranch and his industry since he took over the family business 55 years ago. His land is now etched with more than 40 miles of road, permitting jeeps and trucks to maneuver into areas that, until just a few years ago, only horses could reach. Instead of herds of only white-faced Herefords, he now produces cattle of exotic breeds for hybrid vigor. In response to the desires of health-conscious consumers, his animals are also leaner than ever before.

But Bardin says the biggest change in the beef cattle industry is the result of dwindling numbers of feed lots and packing plants in the state of California: Local cattlemen are forced to truck their animals back east to facilities in Kansas and Iowa where they're fattened, slaughtered, and shipped

The Jim Bardin Hospital was built in 1906 on the corner of John and South Main streets for the City of Salinas by James Bardin II.

back for sale.

"It's truly a revolution in the business," says Bardin. "On Vernon Avenue in Los Angeles there used to be slaughterhouse after slaughterhouse. Now there are practically none. Swift left California 10 or 12 years ago. Armour's gone. The small packing plants that used to be our best friends are just gone. It's cheaper today to ship the steers to the grain than it is to ship the grain to the steers."

One thing that hasn't changed, according to Bardin, is the respect given to a cattleman. "People still kind of look up to cattlemen as being glamorous. You get to work outdoors and ride around on a horse just like the Marlboro Man. I suppose it looks good when you're stuck indoors all day long.

"Now it's true that I like being outside, not confined. And there's a great pride in raising animals that I find very rewarding. But when

you get a cow down and maybe she can't have her calf and you're wading up to your knees and elbows in manure and everything else, it's really not what I would call glamorous; it's just plain work."

In 1940 Bardin built the house in which he and his family now live from lumber taken from a collapsed redwood barn. At that time he was married to Laurine Nissen of Salinas, who died in 1956. Bardin's second wife, Mary, was killed in a ranch jeep accident in 1970, and his son, Robert, died of leukemia in 1983. He is currently married to Dorothy Swanson of Hollister. Through Dorothy, Bardin has three stepchildren: Robert, Lillian, and Margaretta.

Throughout his many years as

a Salinas Valley farmer and rancher, Jim Bardin has been active in both his community and his industry. In 1935 he was elected the first president of the Monterey County Cattlemen's Association, and he has served as first vice-president of the California Cattlemen's Association. He is a former president of the Monterey County Tax Council, a past foreman of the Monterey County Grand Jury, and he served for 25 years on the Water Advisory Commission of the Salinas Valley. During the past 50 years he has been director, and is now president, of the Farmers Mercantile Company of Salinas. He has also been a director of the California Rodeo for 53 years.

At the time of this writing Jim Bardin is 80 years old and still rides the range with his stepdaughter, caring for his cattle as he has done all his life.

JEROME KASAVAN ASSOCIATES, INC.

Above: The Poppy Hills Golf Course club house at Pebble Beach is typical of Jerome Kasavan Associates' excellence in design. Photo by Ron Starr

Left: Jerome Kasavan, AIA.

After earning his architectural degree in 1941 at the University of California, Berkeley, Jerome Kasavan, AIA, served with the Armed Forces in Europe during World War II.

At the end of the war he returned to Salinas to practice his trade and in 1949 founded Jerome Kasavan Associates, Inc., which is today the oldest continually operating architectural firm in Salinas.

His one-man, one-room operation was located upstairs in the old Farmer's Mercantile Building, which currently houses the Dick Bruhn clothing store.

By 1952 Kasavan had expanded his operation into a larger office space on Winham Street and hired a second architect, a draftsman, and a secretary. The company grew steadily over the next 10 years, and Kasavan moved again in 1963, sharing a building on Salinas Street with his brother Herman's accounting firm, Kasavan & Pope. Ten years later Kasavan designed the Hayward Office Building on Romie Lane and moved his business to that location.

Since its founding, Kasavan's firm, recognized for design and business excellence, has designed and seen built more than 600 buildings of diverse size and type. This list includes more than 50 private homes, eight banks, hospitals, post offices, fire houses, and hundreds of commercial projects.

His office has also designed in excess of one million square feet of educational facilities including North

Salinas and Alisal High Schools and 16 elementary schools. Over a period of approximately 30 years of continual architectural service, Jerome Kasavan Associates master planned the campus and designed the new buildings and grounds at Hartnell Community College.

Since the early 1970s the firm has been a leader in the application of passive and active solar energy systems in Central California, and in 1987 Kasavan traveled to China as an ambassador with People to People to share his expertise in solar energy applications. In 1975 Kasavan's firm designed the solar heat-collection system for Hartnell's Olympic-size swimming pool, making it at that time the largest solar-heated pool in the world.

In 1985 Jerome Kasavan Associates was one of the first firms in the area to acquire and utilize a computer-aided drafting and design (CADD) system and has since added new stations to increase its computer capability, including three-dimensional drawing.

Many architects began their careers training with Jerome Kasavan Associates, including at least nine

who have gone on to become principals in their own firms. Jerome's son, Peter Kasavan, AIA, joined the firm in 1981 and is now a part owner. He holds an undergraduate degree in fine arts, was a union journeyman carpenter and construction foreman for nearly six years and earned his graduate degree in architecture from the University of California, Berkeley, in 1981, exactly 40 years after Jerome's graduation.

Jerome, Peter, and Jerome Kasavan Associates' professional staff continues the firm's tradition of producing the highest-quality design, which has made this diverse and well-rounded practice an architectural leader for more than 40 years.

Hartnell College's Classroom Administration Building. Jerome Kasavan Associates, Inc., designed the building and master planned the entire campus. Photo by Ron Starr

MILL CONSTRUCTION COMPANY

From left: Thomas D. Mill, Thomas H. Mill, and company architect Dale Taylor.

When Mill Construction Company president Tom Mill's father first came to the Salinas Valley to work as a carpenter, he had hopes of one day owning his own construction firm. But he probably didn't expect it to grow into a $13-million operation.

It was November 1945 and World War II had just ended when carpenter Thomas H. Mill set foot in Salinas for the first time. Mill had packed up his family and moved from their home in Butte, Montana, to accept a job offer from a Salinas contractor named Ernest Lunt. Mill had worked for Lunt in Pocatello, Idaho, during the war, and the contractor asked him to come to California after the fighting was over.

Mill worked for Lunt and others in the area on both commercial and industrial projects until he earned his contractor's license in 1949. His new construction company specialized in custom-built

*In 1988 Mill built the $4.5-million, 43,000-square-foot **Monterey Herald** production facility. Located in the Monterey Research Park, the facility features a 47-foot-high by 163-foot-long press bay, precast exterior wall panels of glass fiber reinforced concrete, and a structural steel frame.*

homes and cabinets, and quickly earned a reputation for high-quality work and integrity. All of the homes he constructed are still standing in the area around Salinas and including the Pebble Beach area. Mill's business prospered as his reputation grew, but there was one thing missing: his son, Tom.

Tom Mill had graduated from Hartnell College and was completing a degree in civil engineering at the University of California at Berkeley while the Korean War was heating up. He was drafted in November 1953, interrupting his education in his senior year.

Tom spent two years in the army, stationed in Berlin, Germany, then returned home to finish his degree at the University of California at Berkeley. Despite his father's continual offers to join him in Salinas, he remained in the San Francisco Bay Area as a structural/construction engineer working with a former engineering classmate who had started a general contracting company.

It wasn't until 1966, after nine years in the Bay Area, that Tom finally accepted his father's offer and returned to Salinas, where the

two formed a partnership.

Their agreement stated that Tom would take over the management, estimating, and business end of the company, and that the senior Mill would control the construction end in the field. The agreement worked well. In time, Tom shifted the focus of the business away from residential to commercial/industrial, thus helping the firm grow and prosper. A few years later they incorporated.

Thomas Mill retired from Mill Construction Company in 1975, but stayed involved in the business as

The largest broccoli-processing plant in the world (above) was built by Mill Construction for Mann Packing Company, Inc. This $4.5-million contract called for the construction of a 92,000-square-foot building featuring cooler rooms, a processing area (right), an ice production facility, and corporate offices.

a consultant. He also continued to do odd jobs for his personal accounts until his death in 1979.

Unlike most general contractors, Mill Construction is a selling company for which 50 to 60 percent of its business comes from repeat customers. Nearly 80 percent of the firm's contracts involve design work as well as construction.

Mill Construction has successfully completed several important projects in the Monterey, Santa Cruz, and San Benito County area, including the $3.5-million *Herald* printing facility; the new $1.5-million United Parcel Service distribution center; the $5.5-million Tanimura and Antle produce cooling and distribution center; and a $6-million broccoli-processing plant (the largest in the world) for Mann Packing Company. The firm also acted as construction manager for the building of the Barnyard Shopping Center in Carmel.

Mill Construction has an experienced and qualified team of 25 perma-

nent employees that makes the company work. The three key managers are: Mike Black, an 11-year employee who holds a degree in construction engineering from Cal Poly, is the firm's vice-president/contracts and estimating; Bill Taylor, vice-president/construction, who went through the carpenter's apprentice program with Thomas Mill and has been with the organization for 24 years; and Dotti Dunlap, who has served as controller for 11 years.

One of the Mill Construction's specialties is metal buildings. It specializes in metal systems for

commercial/industrial structures and utilizes its own steel erecting crews and equipment. The firm's knowledge of these systems is often custom-applied for multistory, multishaped combinations.

Ernie Mill now works with his father, marking the third generation to join the business. Ernie graduated from Cal Poly with a degree in construction management engineering and worked for two years in Hawaii as a high-rise building estimator and project manager before coming to work with his father. Ernie was the project manager for both the *Herald* and U.P.S. projects, as well as a recent addition to the *Salinas Californian* newspaper facility. His experience and expertise with modern computer technology has helped to bring Mill Construction Company into the computer age.

The business Thomas H. Mill founded 40 years ago has grown and changed over the years. But the reputation for integrity, quality, and professionalism he established remains unchanged.

One of Mill's recent projects was a Tanimura and Antle facility in Spreckels. This $5.5-million contract called for a 40,000-square-foot cooler, a 200-foot by 80-foot shipping dock (shown), storage buildings, and a dispatch office.

MANN PACKING COMPANY

Harold "Cy" Mann elevated broccoli from relative obscurity to what nutritionists today call a "super vegetable" by promoting the commodity rather than his company.

Harold "Cy" Mann, founder of Mann Packing Company, began packaging and shipping broccoli when the vegetable was virtually unknown to the average American consumer. But he knew the sturdy green was a good product and that it would sell. He also knew that with broccoli he had found his niche in the Salinas Valley produce industry.

When the 22-year-old Mann graduated from Stanford University in 1930, he found himself in the middle of the Great Depression with no job and no prospects. He decided, therefore, to travel south to visit a friend—a football coach living in Salinas. "I told him to find me a job or I'd stay and eat off his table," says Mann.

His friend obliged, and it wasn't long before the industrious young Mann was loading cars at a local grain company. He later worked for a while as a fruit trimmer, and then trimmed lettuce for 40 cents an hour.

"Back then," says Mann, "there was no such thing as a company that was recruiting. We all just took what we could get and were glad to get it."

Soon Mann worked his way up to the position of packing shed foreman. He eventually became a buyer for the Arena Company and by 1939 had acquired a broad and varied background in the produce business.

That year Mann decided to use this background to start his own produce company. He called it simply H.W. Mann and began packing and shipping carrots and lettuce from a rented packing house on East Gabilan Street.

At that time the Salinas Valley was filled with many smaller growers who weren't producing for any particular packer; crops were simply grown and offered for sale. So Mann found himself alongside 70 to 80 other packers trading in the fields and trading in the packinghouses. The reputation for honesty and straight dealing Mann earned in those early days helped him to establish strong and loyal relationships with many growers—relationships that have continued into second and third generations.

Mann made the decision to begin packing and shipping broccoli in 1945, at the tail end of World War II. At that time the green was considered strictly an ethnic specialty, eaten mainly by Italian Americans, and the only real markets for it were in New York and Philadelphia. But Mann recognized the potential of a good product with few competitors and began his marketing campaign.

He knew that the first thing he would have to do was educate consumers about broccoli. He began by directing his marketing efforts to elementary schoolteachers, home economists, and registered dieticians. His advertising budget was low, so there was no radio/TV media blitz—no animated broccoli singing the company name. In fact, there was no company name at all. Mann's strategy was to market his commodity, not his company. It was a strategy that would serve him well for 25 years and influence future commodity marketing practices.

The growth of the frozen-food industry at the end of World War II gave Mann's broccoli marketing efforts an unexpected boost by exposing a lot of people to a product they had never had the opportunity to see fresh. When an unknown vegetable appeared on freezer shelves it was in a package bearing cooking instructions for the uninitiated homemaker. Consumers who had never heard of broccoli could simply follow the directions and add a little variety to their dinner menus.

In 1955 Mann moved his operation to the Spiegl Food complex, then located on Abbott Street, and went exclusively into broccoli production. The firm was incorporated at that time and the name was changed.

Though Mann supervised the harvesting and packing at his operation during the early years, made the sales calls, and wrote the paychecks virtually by himself, his company was no longer a one-man business. Indeed, much of the firm's early success depended on Mann's loyal and hardworking staff, among whom were Mann's current partners, Bill Ramsey and Don Nucci.

In 1958 William "Bill" Ramsey was fresh out of the navy, living in Salinas with his wife and child and looking for temporary work until he could return to college. Mann knew Ramsey's father-in-law and called to ask if Bill's brother, Buck, was available to help with the winter broccoli harvest. On his father-in-law's recommendation Mann hired Bill instead. Though Ramsey is currently president of the company, Mann still refers to him as "the temporary employee."

Don Nucci was hired by Ramsey in 1967 as office manager. Nucci, who holds an MBA from the University of California at Berkeley, had spent several years in unsatisfying jobs with the Ford Motor Company and Firestone. When Ramsey offered him a job, Nucci was selling real estate and insurance in Salinas and jumped at the chance for a regular paycheck.

Mann, Ramsey, and Nucci are equal partners in the company today. Ramsey is primarily responsible for growing, harvesting, and cooling operations while Nucci, whose official title is secretary/treasurer, mainly handles finance, personnel, and marketing. Mann is still at his desk every day and is officially the company's board chairman but prefers to call himself "vice-president of something or other."

In June 1981 the Mann Packing operation moved to a new, multimillion-dollar building at 1250 Hansen Street. The new facility houses two ice plants, a massive cold room, cooling and loading facilities, packing and processing facilities, and a string of sales and administrative offices.

Mann's Hansen Street packing plant, completed in 1981, is one of the largest broccoli-processing facilities in the world. For years Mann Packing occupied a portion of the building at upper left.

In addition to broccoli, Mann Packing Company today handles a range of produce items from lettuce and mixed vegetables to asparagus and brussels sprouts. Its Sunny Shore label is carried on a list of more than 25 commodities and is recognized by produce buyers nationwide.

Broccoli, however, is still Cy Mann's favorite, and his company is still recognized as one of the leading broccoli producers in the United States today.

177

MILLS DISTRIBUTING COMPANY

In the produce business, millions of dollars worth of transactions are consummated daily on the basis of trust, utilizing the telephone as the primary negotiating instrument. To survive in an environment founded on trust, a company's name must be synonymous with integrity. Through 30 years of experience in the produce industry, integrity has been the watchword at Mills Distributing Company.

Basil Mills, founder, first came to the Salinas Valley in April 1953, shortly after serving in the United States Army. He took a job with a produce broker, Walter S. Markham, and worked with him for two years. He then went to work for Royal Packing Company, a local lettuce shipper, and remained there for the next three years.

In 1957, when Royal Packing decided to move its operations to Phoenix, Arizona, Basil made the decision to stay in Salinas. In March 1958 he set up his own produce marketing firm, Mills Distributing Company. The faith and confidence of several local growers who wanted him

Among Mills Distributing Company's community contributions was the Special Procedures Room at the Harden Heart Center of the Salinas Valley Memorial Hospital. At the dedication are (from left): Roger E. Mills, Eve Mills, and Basil E. Mills.

Roger E. Mills (left), Basil E. Mills (seated in Model T Ford), and Floyd Griffin survey a lettuce field at the beginning of a harvest. Griffin's Mission Packing Company packs the lettuce shown.

to market their products proved invaluable. Two of those grower-shippers, Cel-a-Pak and Lee & Oshita, gave Basil the cash advance he needed to open a bank account, while a produce broker, Johnny O'Grady, signed a guarantee with the phone company enabling the installation of his telephones—the tools of his trade. Basil has never forgotten the generosity of these individuals and many others who helped him get started.

During the first year of business Basil's younger brother, Roger Mills, joined the firm. He had been attending Indiana State University when Basil offered him a job for the summer. Roger accepted the offer, but made it clear he would stay with the company only long enough to help the fledgling enterprise get off the ground. His goal was to become a CPA, and in the spring of 1959 he went to Arizona to finish his undergraduate studies.

After graduating later that year, Roger returned to the company with a degree in accounting. By 1963 the firm was incorporated,

and Basil gave Roger stock in the new corporation—a decision that encouraged Roger to make the produce business his career. It was a decision, too, that would later make Mills Distributing one of the largest family-run businesses in the industry.

Mills has had many loyal and significant growers as clients through the years. Their first client was Cel-a-Pak, a packer-shipper of cellophane-wrapped cauliflower and one of the produce firms that assisted in getting Mills' company started. After 30 years Mills Distributing still markets Cel-a-Pak's Sassy brand of cauliflower. Hansen Farms, which would eventually become the largest independent grower in California, maintained a close 15-year relationship with the company.

Mission Packing Company, founded by Floyd Griffin in the mid-1970s, turned to Mills for its marketing needs. Today Mission is

one of the premier lettuce shippers in the Salinas Valley and is Mills' largest grower-shipper client.

Beginning in the late 1960s Mills Distributing experienced dramatic growth that has continued through the years. The company had started out by marketing only a mere handful of produce items. Today, with more than 20 individual commodities, the firm markets and moves many times the volume of produce it handled in the early 1960s. From the organization's beginning solely as a marketing company, it is now involved in the growing, packing, and cooling of produce. In addition to the produce sales generated from the Salinas Valley, the firm also ships from Huron, Blythe, and the Imperial Valley of California, as well as Yuma, Arizona.

The Mills' business was founded with a strong sense of family and Christian ethics. Basil is the company's president; brother Roger is vice-president; and Basil's wife, Eve, is secretary/treasurer. Basil's four children have also found successful careers in the business. David Mills is the mixed vegetable sales manager; Jim Mills works in lettuce sales and administration; Kathy Mills works in mixed vegetable sales; and Sue Mills works in accounting and administration. Another great strength and asset of the company is its longtime sales personnel, Ed Little, Marty Martin, and Mark Weber, and its longtime supervisors, Rugena Young and Carol

Brothers Roger (left) and Basil Mills pose with the All-Around Champion Cowboy saddle at the 1988 California Rodeo in Salinas. The saddle is donated yearly by Mills Distributing.

Derbyshire.

The Mills family is active in and supportive of their industry. Basil serves on the board of directors of the Western Growers Association and is a past chairman of the California Iceberg Lettuce Commission. Roger serves as secretary of the Leafy Greens Council. The firm is an involved member of the Grower-Shipper Vegetable Association of Central California, the Produce Marketing Association, the United Fresh Fruit and Vegetable Association, the Central California Lettuce Producers Cooperative, and the Canadian Fruit Wholesalers Association.

The company and family members are also involved in the Salinas community, participating and lending support to the California Rodeo, the California International Airshow, and Sportsfest, a program that focuses on racial harmony in the community. For many years, the first prize awarded to the All-Around Champion Cowboy at the California Rodeo has been a hand-tooled leather saddle donated by

Mills Distributing Company. The family has lent support and served in leadership roles in YMCA, area Rotary clubs, hospital foundations, and several other local charities. Eve Mills is a volunteer in the Valley Guild, which operates the nationally known Steinbeck House.

The Mills family has built their business on the principles of loyalty, integrity, and excellence—principles that emanate from their strong Christian faith. They consider it a privilege to work in the produce industry that produces the bountiful crops that contribute to the health and well-being of all. The produce industry receives no government subsidies and truly exemplifies the free enterprise system, the backbone of this great country.

It is Mills Distributing Company's hope and desire to continue to merit the confidence of its growers and customers and meet the challenges of a demanding and ever-changing industry, while being an integral part of the business sector of the Salinas Valley for generations to come.

From left to right are Jim, Basil, Kathy, Sue, Dave, and Roger Mills with the 1988 Salinas Business Excellence Award for Agribusiness.

PIINI REALTY

During the past 50 years Joe Piini has seen Salinas grow from a small agricultural community into a city of nearly 100,000; but he's done more than just observe that development. As one of the Salinas Valley's foremost real estate firms, Piini Realty has taken an active part in shaping the city of Salinas into what it is today.

The Piini family moved to Soledad from their home in Switzerland in 1927, when young Joe was only eight years old. He later attended Gonzales High School and graduated from Healds Business College in San Jose.

After graduation Joe worked pitching hay in various ranches around Soledad and Gonzales. His mother asked John Breschini, a distant relative who worked for local attorney-turned-realtor George Gould, to help her son land a job in real estate.

"When I started working in Mr. Gould's office," says Joe, "he made sure I understood that he would pay me $65 for the first month and, if I did well, I'd get a raise to $75. If I didn't do well,

Reviewing plans for the 105-lot Country Meadows subdivision are (from left): Chip Campion, Jim Piini, Joe Piini, and John Piini.

that would be the end of it."

But Joe did very well for Gould. His first sale, in 1939, was a home on five acres in the Corral de Tierra area for $2,000—a home that would probably sell for $300,000 today.

In May 1941 Joe entered the navy and served until the end of World War II. One month later he married Maxine Medeiros of Hollister, to whom he has remained married for 47 years.

While Joe was away from his job, Gould died, and John Breschini took over the office. When he got out of the service Joe went to work for Breschini and stayed with the firm for the next 25 years until 1970, when he built his own office.

In 1950 Joe became the first MAI (Member of the American Institute of Appraisers) in Salinas. During the 1950s and 1960s he was

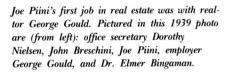

Joe Piini's first job in real estate was with realtor George Gould. Pictured in this 1939 photo are (from left): office secretary Dorothy Nielsen, John Breschini, Joe Piini, employer George Gould, and Dr. Elmer Bingaman.

the biggest developer of residential property in the area, with more than 750 lots in Salinas to his credit.

Though none of Joe and Maxine's children had originally planned to go into real estate, Piini Realty has always been a family business. Jim Piini studied finance in Santa Clara and planned to work for one of the large companies in the valley when he decided he would rather work in a small organization. He joined the family firm in 1971. John Piini graduated from UCLA in 1974 and was headed for law school when he joined the firm. He obtained his MAI designation in 1983. Chip Campion, who is married to Joine Piini, graduated from UCLA in 1972 and was ready for graduate school there when he accepted Joe's job offer.

Joe has been very active in his community, plying his trade for more than profit. He was instrumental in acquiring and helping to generate financing for the Madonna del Sasso school and parish in North Salinas, and he helped raise money for the purchase of property for Palma and Notre Dame high schools. He renovated the old Masonic Temple, where Gadsby's Music is located today, making him one of the first to become involved in downtown redevelopment. He also helped the Valley Guild buy the Steinbeck House.

But Joe says that his greatest achievement can't be measured by a property line. "It was very important to have my children come into the business," says Joe. "To me, that was my most important accomplishment."

JOHN PRYOR COMPANY

Because of John Pryor's innovations, liquid fertilizer has become the dominant form used in modern growing operations. Here, Pryor stands next to the tanks used in the application of liquid fertilizer.

They don't call it the Salad Bowl for nothing. From May to September nearly 10 million heads of lettuce are shipped daily from the Salinas Valley to markets throughout the United States. Much of that huge crop is grown with the help of the liquid fertilizer technology pioneered by the John Pryor Company.

When Pryor first arrived in the Salinas Valley, the vast majority of growers were still using dry fertilizers. After graduating from the University of California at Davis with a degree in plant science, he worked in Fresno for the University of California Agricultural Extension Service. In 1940 he left that job to do seed and fertilizer research for Growers Ice and Development Company in Salinas.

By 1946 Pryor's research had led him to the conclusion that the rarely used liquid fertilizers he was studying had the potential to virtually replace the more popular dry types. He saw how growers could inject the liquid product into their irrigation systems for a more efficient operation.

He also saw an opportunity. That same year Pryor left Growers

Ice, determined to establish one of the area's first liquid fertilizer companies.

To get his enterprise off the ground Pryor needed $30,000—an enormous sum in those days. So, with an abundance of confidence and a shortage of collateral, Pryor approached Bruce Church, grandfather of the lettuce industry and one of the founders of Growers Ice. Church was impressed with Pryor's idea and made him an unsecured loan for the entire amount. (Though Pryor's great friend and benefactor has since died, Church's company remains an important and continuous user of John Pryor Company fertilizer.)

With his financing firmly in hand, Pryor soon began operations. But the liquid fertilizer industry was brand new, and equipment for application was practically nonexistent. Starting with only one employee, Pryor trucked 50-gallon drums of his liquid fertilizer into

the fields and injected it into growers' irrigation systems himself. Years later the company would be applying fertilizer to nearly 230,000 crop acres every year. It would also develop one of the industry's first side-dressing tractors for liquid fertilizer.

Pryor's idea was an immediate success with growers from one end of the valley to the other, and he managed to finish that first year in the black—or so he thought. Though his company has made a profit every year since, he recalls how, at

The Pryor Company helped pioneer the use of side-dressing tractors for liquid fertilization. Photo circa 1963

the end of his first year of operation, his accountant's report of a year-end profit turned out to be a mistake. The firm had, in fact, lost money. "But the error," says Pryor, "was awfully good for morale."

Today liquid fertilizer has become the dominant variety used in most modern growing operations. The John Pryor Company, with plants in Salinas and Soledad, is recognized nationwide as one of the most innovative and best-managed firms in the industry.

STONE CONTAINER CORPORATION

Since its founding more than 33 years ago, the Salinas Valley manufacturing plant of the Stone Container Corporation has done more than just make good boxes. It has evolved a specialized plant within the corrugated industry, working beside local growers and shippers to develop products and services that have become the standard for produce packaging throughout the country.

Produced by Growers Container Corporation beginning in April 1956, the first cauliflower case manufactured featured cellophane wraps color-matched to the brand.

Originally called Growers Container Corporation, the firm was established by a group of Salinas Valley grower/shippers in 1954, slightly more than a year after vacuum cooling began to revolutionize the lettuce industry. The new cooling process had eliminated the need to pack head lettuce in wooden crates piled high with ice, and the growers wanted to manufacture their own corrugated boxes.

In addition to lettuce producers, the company attracted growers with additional commodities that did not require icing, such as potatoes, tomatoes, apples, and citrus fruits. But owing to the seasonal nature of agriculture, the new company eventually branched out and began manufacturing industrial boxes for businesses in the San Fran-

cisco Bay area.

Produce, however, continued to be the focus of the firm's research and development efforts. Since, at that time, only lettuce was being successfully vacuum cooled, most other produce items still required "body ice," which would eventually soak through and break down corrugated board.

Then, in 1959, the company developed a wax-saturated corrugated board called Wet-Lok™. Roughly 50 percent of the corrugated board was saturated with a paraffin wax blend so the product stood up under heavy icing and water. The company then began making boxes for an increasing number of other wet commodities.

As the company began to grow, and in order to service the needs of growers' southern operations during the winter months, Growers Container built a plant in Fullerton and later built another plant in Florida.

The company was at a disadvantage without its own paper mills to

supply linerboard and medium; it was sold to St. Regis in 1960. St. Regis was a fully integrated paper company with its own paper mills. For almost eight years the Salinas plant benefited from a steady supply of good, quality materials from the firm's new owner.

In 1967 the corrugated box manufacturer had a new owner: Hoerner-Waldorf Corporation. This was a strong, family-owned firm headquartered in the Midwest, with a good timber base in Missoula, Montana.

During its Hoerner-Waldorf period, the Salinas plant continued to manufacture a diversified line of products, producing roughly 60 percent of its boxes for the agricultural industry and 40 percent for industrial clients. Hoerner-Waldorf also purchased a plant in San Jose that specialized in manufacturing industrial packaging, and the Salinas plant shifted 95 percent of its efforts to agriculture.

Growers Container Corporation's Salinas headquarters, circa 1956.

Among Growers Container's 1956 board of directors were (seated, left to right): R.L. Vayo, W.R. Adams, and Bruce Church. Standing from left are: Jack Abramson, Larry Kurz, Tom McNamara, John Cowles, G.L. Dales, John Martin, Ted Nelson, Lindsey Cochran, Bill Garin, Russ Merrill, Gene Harden, Harry Richardson, Karl Christierson, Tony Resetar, P.W. Williams, E.W. Milsted, Andy D'Arrigo, and Frank Bennett. Directors not shown include: Bud Antle, V.M. Arena, Ray Eaton, Frank Hogue, Ed Martori, Ken Nutting, and Peter A. Stolich.

In 1978 the company was purchased by Champion International. During the next nine years, the firm made its greatest inroads into produce packaging. Along with advances in produce cooling technology, corrugated boxes played a more important role. Today virtually all fresh vegetables are shipped in some type of corrugated container.

Finally, in February 1986, Stone Container Corporation acquired Champion International. The new owner is another family firm with a long history in the paper industry. The multibillion-dollar corporation has more than 20,000 employees and some 150 facilities across the United States. It is the largest producer and converter of unbleached paper and paperboard container packaging in the world.

The management at Stone's home office recognized that its newly acquired Salinas operation was unique. Unlike its other plants, the Salinas plant had to live and breathe agriculture. As Stone Container likes to do with most of its manufacturing plants, local managers have the full authority to run the manufacturing operation.

In Salinas that kind of decentralized management has lead to pioneering industry innovations such as: Maxaire venting for fresh vegetable packaging, standard container and pallet size development (currently adopted by the United Fresh Fruit and Vegetable Association), Titanium ink coating for more attractive brite white graphics and greater heat reflective qualities, plus a number of developments in packaging systems with self-locking features for shed and field packing.

Perhaps its more important development is a company that is reliable and easy to do business with. Through five owners and more than 30 years of change and innovation, the Salinas Stone Container operation has maintained a continuous relationship with all of its customers, and continues to break new ground and set new standards in fresh agricultural packaging.

All over the world produce consumers are familiar with boxes manufactured by Stone Container Corporation. Shown here is the 1988 product line.

ARROW LETTUCE COMPANY

Arrow Lettuce Company has seen many changes since it was founded in 1934—changes in its operations, personnel, and even the company name. But through it all one thing has remained constant: The name "Musante" is still on the company masthead.

The company founder was George B. Musante, the son of Italian immigrants who settled in New York City at the turn of the century. Musante began working in the produce business in 1919 in the well-known Washington Street produce market there.

Later he worked as a buyer for a wholesale produce receiver, traveling to several states around the country and eventually to California. It was during his first trip to the Golden State that Musante de-

From left to right are Nancy Orozco, office manager; Dana Musante, receptionist; Lowry Backus, vice-president; and Dick Musante, president.

George B. Musante (front left in white coat) is shown in 1919 at the famous Washington Street produce market in New York City. He began operations as Musante Williams in Salinas in 1934; twelve years later it was renamed Arrow Lettuce Company.

cided to forsake New York for San Jose, then a major center of the agriculture industry.

By 1934 Musante had ventured into the up-and-coming new produce center, Salinas. At that time he and his close friend Ralph Coelho, already in business together as Pacific Farm Company in San Jose, joined with P.W. Williams to form Musante Williams, Inc.

During the next 12 years Musante and Coelho would have a number of partners, changing the company name with each addition or subtraction. Finally, in 1946, they changed the name permanently to Arrow Lettuce Company.

Though Dick Musante has

worked in various aspects of agriculture for most of his life and is president of Arrow Lettuce today, he never got a chance to work with his father. A year after Musante had graduated from the University of Santa Clara in 1951, his father died. Musante then spent the next two years in the United States Air Force.

While Musante was in the service, Coelho continued to operate the Arrow Lettuce Company. When his stint with the air force was finished, Musante began at Arrow by working in various company operations for Coelho and general manager Leonard Cling, who became a partner in 1964 and died in 1976.

Coelho was a good teacher and became a sort of second father to the young Musante. Even after he had ceased active management of the company, Ralph Coelho played an important role in the success of Arrow Lettuce until his death in 1986.

The company, which is currently owned and operated by Dick Musante, Miles Holaday, and Lowry Backus, has made several changes during the years. The firm began as a shipper but added a farming operation in 1957. All company operations, which had been scat-

Left: From left: Miles Holaday, corporate secretary; Oscar Gardea, broccoli harvesting supervisor; Mario Cruz, cauliflower harvesting supervisor; and George Musante, Jr., harvesting foreman.

Right: They keep things rolling: shop foreman Clarence King (left), with Joe Sigala and Joe Martinez.

tered around several area ranches, were consolidated in 1976 into a new facility at 1375 Burton Avenue in Salinas. Though the firm's original specialty was lettuce, Arrow currently focuses its efforts on the harvesting and marketing of broccoli, cauliflower, and mixed vegetables.

Arrow Lettuce Company operates year-round in the Salinas Valley. The company harvests broccoli year-round, while cauliflower is harvested roughly five months a year. "We are planting and harvesting almost every day of the year," says Dick Musante.

Lowry Backus and Miles Holaday, both principals of the company, combining 62 years of experience in produce, contract with growers and carefully schedule planting dates with the numerous growers throughout the Salinas Valley to produce 45 to 50 million pounds of product annually.

Oscar Gardea, a 15-year vet-

Arrow Lettuce has a fleet of seven broccoli harvesting machines, one of which is pictured here. In addition to broccoli, these implements harvest cauliflower.

eran with the company, supervises all the broccoli harvesting and coordinates deliveries to processors and shipping agents. Currently the company is supplying product to four different frozen-food processors.

Mario Cruz, also a 15-year veteran, supervises and coordinates all cauliflower harvesting and deliveries.

But even with all the changes, the company continues as a close-knit organization, ushering in the younger generation with the recent additions of George Musante, Jr., Bill Backus, and Dana Musante.

"Hopefully we will be going for another 50 years," says Musante.

185

D'ARRIGO BROS. COMPANY

When D'Arrigo Bros. Company founders Andrew and Stephen D'Arrigo emigrated from Messina, Italy, in the early part of this century, they had little education and spoke no English. Even with these handicaps, however, they managed to create a company that would become a major influence in the development of Salinas Valley agriculture.

Andrew D'Arrigo arrived in Boston, Massachusetts, in 1904 and went to work in the local woolen mills. His younger brother, Stephen, followed in 1911. They later earned their American citizenship and served in the U.S. Armed Forces during World War I.

After the war the two brothers went to work in their cousins' grape juice business, with Andrew remaining in the East and Stephen moving to California to supervise shipments from the West Coast. By 1922 the two brothers terminated their partnership with their cousins and formed the D'Arrigo Bros. Company.

D'Arrigo Bros., under Stephen, began as a produce specialty company in San Jose, growing and shipping a variety of fruits and vegetables favored by Italian-Americans. In addition to sweet anise and cactus pears, the firm imported Pascal celery seed from Nice, France, which yielded the first crop of its kind ever grown in California.

However, it was with broccoli that D'Arrigo Bros. really found its niche in the California agriculture industry: The young firm was the first U.S. produce company to commercially grow, pack, and ship the now-popular vegetable from the West Coast. Broccoli was so unknown in the industry when they first began planting it that the brothers had to develop their own seed lines, planting seed sent to them by their father from Italy.

According to a study published

Brothers Stephen (above) and Andrew D'Arrigo (left) arrived in the United States from Italy in 1911 and 1904, respectively, to seek their destiny in the New World. In 1922 they formed D'Arrigo Bros. Company.

in the *Harvard Marketing Review,* D'Arrigo Bros. was also the first company to successfully employ brand identification principles of product items. Using a photograph of Stephen's son, current president Andrew D'Arrigo, taken at age two, the firm developed the Andy Boy label to promote sales of its broccoli crops. The company still uses the label on all its premium products.

Today D'Arrigo Bros. is a full-service, vertically integrated produce firm, farming 14,000 acres in California and Arizona. It harvests, packs, and markets 39 different crops throughout the year. The crops are sold from company facilities in California and Arizona, and through company outlets in Boston and New York.

In the East, the D'Arrigo Bros. Company of New York is directed by co-founder Andrew D'Arrigo's older son, Stephen D'Arrigo. D'Arrigo Bros. Company of Massachusetts is managed by his younger son, Peter D'Arrigo.

The D'Arrigo Bros. Company

D'Arrigo Bros. Company was the first produce company to successfully use product identification principles. Here, in this 1945 photo, workers are using a paper label identifying wrap and twistem to label broccoli with the Andy Boy label.

of California is now in its third generation with president Andrew D'Arrigo's children, John, David, and Marrianne D'Arrigo, joining in the family business.

Andrew and Stephen D'Arrigo had nothing but courage and ambition when they left their homeland more than 80 years ago. However, the company they founded remains an influential force in American agriculture.

MCCORMICK & COMPANY
MCCORMICK-SCHILLING DIVISION

The new Schilling plant began operation in the Salinas Valley in 1967. An earlier facility was burned down during the Great San Francisco Earthquake.

The Schilling Division of McCormick & Company formally dedicated its 300,000-square-foot Salinas plant on May 19, 1967, marking the 20th anniversary of the merging of A. Schilling & Co. with McCormick & Co.

Schilling's first plant was opened in 1881 by two ambitious young German immigrants: August Schilling and George Volkmann, who started their own coffee, tea, and spice business near the San Francisco waterfront.

In those days it was common practice within that industry to adulterate products. Chicory, rice, and other grains went into coffee, and tea was dyed green to make it more attractive to housewives. Schilling considered these methods unethical, and, though there were no laws to force them to do so, they began packaging pure, unadulterated coffee and tea in 1890 with no price increases. Sixteen years later the Pure Food and Drug Act would force their competitors to do the same.

Following 22 years of successful operation, the company moved into a new plant at Second and Folsom streets in 1903. Three years later that facility was destroyed by fire during the Great San Francisco Earthquake.

Schilling continued production

at other locations in New York and Portland, Oregon. The company's familiar slogan, "Schilling's Best," was modified for awhile to "After the fire, this is the nearest we can get to Schilling's Best." A year later a new facility was constructed where the old one stood, and operations continued as before.

In 1947 the firm merged with the Baltimore-based McCormick & Co., adopting the new slogan, "United to serve the nation's good taste." The merger was so successful that by the 1960s the San Francisco factory was just too small to accommodate the increasing West Coast sales volume.

In 1966, after first considering locations in both Fresno and Santa Barbara, construction of a new plant on a 20-acre site at Harkins and Hansen roads in Salinas began, with operations commencing one

year later.

Following the merger Schilling had operated as a separate division of McCormick. In 1977, however, it was integrated with another McCormick division to form what is now the McCormick-Schilling Division.

Today the Salinas plant manufactures the bottled and canned spices, seasoning blends, and Mexican dinners sold under the Schilling label. It also packages products sold under private labels. The spice-processing department cleans, mills, and blends the products for the packaging operations, and helps support the production requirements for the Food Service and Flavor divisions.

The success of the McCormick-Schilling Division of McCormick & Co. has been based on its uncompromising attention to quality in raw materials and packaging, and its attention to detail at every step of the operation. More than 100 years later August Schilling's commitment to produce ". . . pure products, in full weight packages, honestly advertised, and honestly sold" is being carried on.

The people who comprise Schilling celebrate 100 years of producing ". . . pure products, in full weight packages, honestly advertised, and honestly sold."

THE CASTROVILLE ARTICHOKE PEOPLE

Not many years ago few visitors would have recognized the elephant-size, spiky, green globe sculpture standing at the east end of Castroville—let alone imagined a smaller version of it on their dinner plates. But thanks to the efforts of The Castroville Artichoke People (CAP), that sculpture—and the thistle-turned-vegetable it represents—is becoming as familiar to American consumers as mom's apple pie.

CAP was formed in 1987, when several longtime local artichoke producers decided to combine forces to promote the superior Castroville artichoke. Its membership includes four grower/shippers: Associated Produce Distributors, Boggiatto Packing Company, D'Arrigo Bros. Company, and The California Artichoke and Vegetable Growers Corporation, as well as the nation's only artichoke processor, Artichoke Industries.

Castroville has been the center of the American artichoke industry ever since Angelo Del Chiaro moved his farming operation from Pescadero to the Central Coast in

1921. Del Chiaro and the growers who followed him found that the fertile soil of the Salinas River Valley and the cool, foggy climate created there by breezes skimming the Monterey Bay formed an environment perfect for growing artichokes.

Today all but 500 of the more than 12,000 acres planted in artichokes nationwide are located between Half Moon Bay and Santa Barbara, with the Castroville area the highest producer in the nation.

The citizens of Castroville celebrate the vegetable that is the heart of their economy with an annual festival. Though it started out as something resembling a church picnic among grower families, the Castroville Artichoke Festival has grown into an impressive event, with a parade, a street fair, and an artichoke queen. The community's first artichoke queen was none other than Marilyn Monroe, who was crowned while in the area on a promotional tour in 1947.

The festival is but one way in which the artichoke is honored. Castroville is also the site of a monu-

Some Castroville Artichoke People pose beneath the famous Castroville sign.

ment to that vegetable— *The Giant Artichoke*—that stands year round. The steel-and-plaster goliath was built in 1963 to adorn a fruit and vegetable market, now owned by longtime Castroville resident Ray Bei. The giant artichoke stands 20 feet tall, measures 12 feet across, and is a popular photo subject with tourists.

At the restaurant next door hungry visitors can choose from a menu of artichoke dishes ranging from soup to quiche, from omelettes to cake.

Through the years the growers and shippers of the community of Castroville have continued to bring to market the finest artichokes possible. The Castroville Artichoke People are aware of the needs of that market and strive to meet them, setting the standard to which all California artichoke growers and shippers aspire.

FIRST NATIONAL BANK OF MONTEREY COUNTY

First National Bank of Monterey County began its banking operation on April 2, 1984, with offices in both Salinas and Monterey. This unique decision to open two offices simultaneously has helped First National serve a broad base of customers and shareholders throughout Monterey County.

Pacific Capital Bancorp, the holding company for First National Bank, was founded by local business and civic leaders with countless years of experience in the two communities. From its founding First National Bank has been independently operated by a staff of highly experienced banking professionals.

The Salinas banking office, located at 1001 South Main Street, was remodeled in 1984 to reflect a modern banking environment. The bank's Administration Center opened in November 1985 in the old Globe Theatre building on South Main Street, and moved to the 300 block of Main Street in the spring of 1989. The new facility houses the bank's state-of-the-art computer system and administrative offices, as well as training center and community room.

The Monterey banking operation began in downtown Monterey in the historic Casa Madariaga adobe, which now serves as the bank's boardroom and community room, and in 1985 a banking facility was built adjacent to the adobe.

First National began operations with an initial capital investment of $6 million and almost 700 local shareholders and founders. The bank ended its first full year of operations with a profit, and its investors received a 5 percent stock dividend in August of 1985.

1001 South Main Street is home to the Salinas Banking Office of First National Bank of Monterey County.

Due to the substantial early growth, First National launched a secondary stock offering in the spring of 1987, increasing its shareholder base to more than 1,000 persons.

First National Bank has continued to enjoy steady, controlled growth and has consistently ranked among the most profitable independent banks in California. First National has been named recipient of the prestigious "Premier Performing Bank" award every year since its inception by The Findley Reports, a leading California bank consulting firm.

The bank's continued growth and profits are a direct result of the focus on its high-quality loan portfolio. First National remains steadfast in its commitment to the local economy of Monterey County.

This commitment is also evidenced by First National's sponsorship of many local community events, its support of a wide variety of nonprofit organizations, and its dedication to providing civic leadership to the communities it serves.

From left: D. Vernon Horton, president; Charles E. Bancroft, founding chairman of the board; and Clayton C. Larson, executive vice-president.

First National Bank continues to play a viable role in the economic, social, and cultural growth of the Salinas Valley and all of Monterey County.

TANIMURA AND ANTLE

The Tanimura and Antle families have been growing, marketing, cooling, and harvesting vegetable crops in the Salinas Valley for more than 40 years. Though their fresh vegetable business is only a few years old, the two families have worked together for most of that time.

In 1952 the Tanimura brothers first entered into a joint venture with Lester "Bud" Antle. The contract called for the Tanimuras to do the growing and for Antle to handle the marketing and shipping of a single acre of iceberg lettuce.

In time, the two family businesses grew. The five Tanimuras— George, Charles, John, Robert, and Tom—and Charles' two sons, Gary and Keith, focused on the management of growing operations while Bud Antle, his son, Robert, and later his grandsons, Rick and Mike, concentrated on their packing and shipping business.

Antle's operation, called Bud Antle, Inc., now known Bud of California, would eventually become the largest vegetable shipper in the Salinas Valley. The Tanimura family would continue expanding its growing operations, contracting with Antle to produce many of the vegetables he would ship.

In 1978 Bud Antle, Inc., merged with Castle & Cook. Following the merger the Tanimuras and Antles continued their grower and shipper relationship until 1982, when the Tanimuras and the Antles decided to combine their talents, experience, and resources to form their own fully integrated growing and shipping company, to be called Tanimura and Antle.

In its first few years T&A farmed in excess of 6,000 acres and shipped nearly 5 million units. By 1987, in the space of only five years, those numbers had grown to more than 12,000 acres and in excess of 12 million units.

Today T&A produces a range of vegetable products including naked and wrapped iceberg lettuce, as well as romaine, green leaf, red leaf, Boston, and Little Gem lettuce. The firm also produces celery, cauliflower, and green onions.

The company's marketing strategy sounds simple: to provide quality products on a consistent basis

The "T&A" brand is the result of Tanimura and Antle's commitment to top-quality, innovative production operations.

to customers who understand their value. But to do that T&A grows on only the finest farmland. On their own farms or with other quality-conscious farmers under joint-venture agreements, Tanimura and Antle produces only the finest products for their quality-conscious customers.

The harvesting and packing operations at T&A continue the company's high standards with the use of innovative equipment and careful scheduling of harvest crews. The firm also maintains a consistent volume of produce by conducting operations in several locations, including Salinas, Huron, Oxnard, California; Yuma, Arizona; and recently, Cuidad Obregon, Mexico.

Since its inception Tanimura and Antle has actively pursued alternative packaging, handling, and product development. T&A was the first company in the area to ship flat-pack lettuce on racks; the first to ship food-service lettuce with the core in, packed in the field; and the first to ship naked palletized lettuce with a poly liner, resulting in re-

duced carton chafe and dehydration, with enhanced product arrivals.

In addition, T&A introduced Little Gem lettuce to North America and developed the latest generation of wrapping machines and transfer-handling systems, both of which have become the industry standard. T&A also developed and patented a resealable taping system for use with bagged lettuce and cauliflower that will have a tremendous impact on the industry.

The company's latest innovation, however, is certainly its biggest. In April 1988 all T&A operations were moved into a 70,000-square-foot cooling facility in Spreckels. The new facility has a 40,000-square-foot cold room, a 10,000-square-foot dry storage area, and 2,500 square feet of office

space. The new operation is located on 18 acres, is surrounded by T&A farmland, and handles 50,000 cartons of produce and 100 trucks daily. In addition, in September 1988 T&A moved its 12,000-square-foot headquarters to this Spreckels location.

Working together and staying involved in all phases of operations, from walking fields and supervising growing and harvesting, to meeting with customers and making certain they get the best-possible product, the Tanimura and Antle families are keeping ahead of the community. T&A is a company that has established and continues to maintain standards that have made it an industry leader.

Tanimura and Antle's new headquarters, completed in 1988, is located in Spreckels.

STEINBECK FEDERAL CREDIT UNION

The founders of the Steinbeck Federal Credit Union were not bankers, C.P.A.s, or wizards of high finance. They were Salinas teachers who banded together to provide for themselves the loan services that the banks would not.

In the early 1950s the children of World War II veterans who, a few years earlier, had returned home to settle down and raise families, were beginning to flood the Salinas school system. The demand for new teachers was tremendous, and nearly half the faculties of area schools consisted of young educators with annual salaries of about $3,600, budding families, and no credit. It was a tough time, indeed, to get started in a new town without help.

On July 18, 1950, a group of eight Salinas teachers signed an organization certificate issued by the Social Security Administration for charter number 6826 and formed one of the Salinas Valley's first credit unions. It was called the Salinas Area Teachers Federal Credit Union, and its membership included Salinas teachers and their families. Its

membership fee was 25 cents, and there was a minimum balance requirement of five dollars. The new credit union approved about $400 weekly in loans for furniture, automobiles, and Christmas presents; they even made a loan to a member who needed a lawyer to get out of jail in Tijuana. The group's first loan was for $200 to repair a roof.

Don Thompson, a mathematics teacher at Washington Junior High School, became the group's first treasurer and manager. During its first three years the credit union was represented in a box in a cupboard at the back of his classroom. Jacque Eyde became the moving spirit behind the organization and the first full-time manager.

The group's first permanent office was established in 1963 at 17 East San Joaquin Street, where the expanded facilities stand today. Its original name was changed in 1979 to Central Coast Schools Federal Credit Union to reflect a membership that now included all area public and parochial school employees.

By June 1984 the credit union

Founded in 1950 by eight Salinas schoolteachers, Steinbeck Federal Credit Union began with a modest 25-cent membership and about $400 in loans approved weekly. Today the credit union boasts $18 million in assets and offers its members a diverse range of services.

had changed its name again and widened its membership to include 40 businesses. Today, with $18 million in assets, membership in the Steinbeck Federal Credit Union is open to employees of more than 2,000 area businesses.

Along with membership expansion, the Steinbeck Federal Credit Union has also expanded its services. In addition to the traditional share accounts, Steinbeck Federal offers regular checking and money market checking. Other services include individual retirement accounts (IRAs), overdraft protection, direct deposits, travelers' checks, insurance discounts, and ATM access.

Though business is no longer conducted out of a shoebox in the back of a schoolroom, the Steinbeck Federal Credit Union is still dedicated to meeting individual financial needs through common sense services tailored to its members.

THE SALINAS CALIFORNIAN

The **Salinas Californian's** *original press, installed in 1949, was replaced in 1986 with a $3.5-million, four-color machine that reproduces full-color photographs.*

In 1869 the tiny community of Salinas had one of the only two newspapers in Monterey County. It was the seed from which grew one of the Central Coast's most important daily newspapers: the *Salinas Californian.*

The *Salinas Valley Standard,* Salinas' first newspaper and the second ever published in Monterey County, started in 1869. It was a four-page weekly put together in a small shack on Gabilan Street behind the Eagle drugstore. The entire operation consisted of an antiquated Hoe-Washington handpress and about 100 pounds of type. Because there wasn't enough type to print all four pages at once, the *Standard* was printed two pages at a time.

In 1871 the *Standard* was replaced by the *Salinas Weekly Index.* After the death of the paper's founder, Melville Byerly, in 1876, the *Index* was sold to W.J. Hill, a well-known newspaperman from Idaho. Hill published and edited the *Index* for the next 33 years.

By 1919 the *Index* had been purchased by Fred Weybret, who later purchased a rival local paper, the *Salinas Daily Journal,* and combined

Completed in 1948, this building at 123 West Alisal Street still houses the **Salinas Californian.**

the two publications in 1928 to form the *Salinas Index-Journal.*

Weybret retired in 1932 and sold the *Index-Journal* to E.L. Sherman, the former owner of the *Modesto News-Herald.* Four years later the paper was sold to Merritt C. Speidel and his associates from Iowa City, Iowa, who were forming a newspaper chain. Within a month that group purchased another local paper, the *Salinas Morning Post,* and formed a new company, Salinas Newspapers, Inc.

In 1937 Paul H. Caswell, former publisher of the *Cherokee* and the *Iowa Daily Times,* came to work for Salinas Newspapers and became publisher of both the *Index-Journal* and the *Post.* Caswell would continue as publisher until his retire-

ment in 1961.

The *Index-Journal* and the *Post* were published mornings, evenings, and Sundays until 1942. But because of wartime restrictions on paper and the general scarcity of manpower and supplies, Salinas Newspapers replaced both publications that year with a single, new evening paper, the *Salinas Californian.* The new publication was a combination of the *Index-Journal* and the *Morning Post.*

At that time the paper was published at 137 Monterey Street, but as the publication grew, plans were made for construction of a new building. The new, two-story facility, located at the southwest corner of Alisal and Church streets, was completed in 1948.

In 1961 Francis H. Cislini became president of the *Californian.* Cislini began his newspaper career as a printer's apprentice at the original *Salinas Index* and retired in 1972, ending 50 years in the business.

Cislini was succeeded by Robert L. Huttenhoff, who continued as publisher until 1984, when Toni Marie Wiggins was named to that position.

Today the *Californian* is a member of the Gannett newspaper organization. The paper is produced in the same building on Alisal Street, but the facility was expanded in 1986 to accommodate a new, $3.5-million four-color press. In early 1987 Wiggins was succeeded by current *Californian* publisher Karen Wittmer. With a circulation exceeding 23,000, Wittmer and *Californian* editor Dave Doucette operate one of the finest and most influential publications in Monterey County.

SALINAS STEEL BUILDERS

Salinas Steel Builders has erected hundreds of thousands of square feet of buildings ranging from offices to schools, from warehouses to retail shops and agricultural buildings. The company has become one of the Salinas Valley's foremost design/build contractors. And it's all because of the dreams and hard work of a young welder from the Midwest.

When he was eight years old, Homer W. Goldman and his family left their home in Kansas to escape the desperate poverty of the Depression-era Dust Bowl. They stopped first in Idaho, where the Goldman children spent several months living in a tent while their homestead cabin was being built. But after two years of more of the same thing they'd left behind in Kansas, Homer's family pulled up stakes and headed for the Golden State.

On arriving in California the Goldmans took up residence in Watsonville, where they made their living in the produce industry. The Goldman family was a very large one, so everyone had to work to make ends meet—even 10-year-old Homer.

Though his education was cut short at the eighth grade, Homer is remembered as an intelligent, hardworking boy with a strong sense of family responsibility. Allen Goldman recalls that his brother would always choose the hot, sunny side of the trees where he and his siblings were picking prunes, so that they could work in the shade.

Homer eventually learned the welding trade working for the AD&H Company during World War II. The welding and metal fabrication company had a shop on Monterey Street in Salinas. Al Heir, one of the owners of AD&H, recalls the young Goldman as one of his best employees—one he was

sorry to lose.

But Homer dreamed of starting his own business and knew he couldn't settle for a job in a welding shop. In 1946 he saw his first opportunity for independence.

The Butler Manufacturing Company had been a major domestic supplier of prefabricated metal buildings during World War II. At the end of the war Butler had a tremendous surplus of these buildings ready for shipping to remote U.S. military outposts.

To help develop a domestic market for these buildings Butler appointed the E.C. Livingston Company to distribute its products throughout the western United States. E.C. Livingston soon discovered a large market for prefabricated metal structures within the agriculture industry in the Salinas Valley, too large

for the company's building crews to handle alone.

This was the opportunity Homer had been looking for, and he quickly found himself erecting Butler Buildings as a subcontractor for the E.C. Livingston Company. He called his new enterprise Homer Goldman Steel Erectors. As his business expanded, Homer's brothers, John and Allen Goldman, came to work for him. For the next 10 years Homer's company focused on steel erection, welding, and fabrication of metal buildings for the farming and industrial communities of Monterey, Santa Cruz, and San Benito counties.

In 1960 he obtained his general contracting license and was awarded the only Butler Building franchise for the Central Coast. The company name was

After four years of working out of his backyard, Homer Goldman set up shop at this site on Vertin Street. Both structures shown were built by Goldman.

changed at that time to Salinas Steel Builders and soon became known as a general contractor for industrial, commercial, and agricultural structures and office buildings.

That year also saw Warren and Harvey Goldman join their father and uncles in the growing business. Harvey began as an iron worker, walking the six-inch highway, and later came into the office as an estimator and salesman.

Homer thought Warren was too big to climb around on steel so he put his son to work as a carpenter's apprentice. Ten years later Warren moved into the office as an estimator, draftsman, and salesman.

The five Goldmans each contributed $500 to buy a piece of property in Sand City in 1960. They

erected a warehouse on that site for leasing and initiated the Warehouse Leasing Company of Goldman Land and Development Co., or Glad, as it is know today.

The Goldman family has since constructed and leased more than 500,000 square feet to nearly 100 businesses in Salinas. Salinas Steel Builders has erected 75 percent of all the multitenant rental warehouse space in Salinas. The company currently performs a wide range of services, from site selection, development, and planning, through final-phase construction and small remodeling projects.

Homer Goldman died in 1979, and his brothers retired from the business two years later. Salinas Steel Builders, however, continues its tradition of family participation with current company president Warren Gold-

man's sons, Jeffery and Stephen Goldman, who are working as estimators/salesmen. Joining the Goldmans at Salinas Steel Builders is a group of skilled professionals, including general manager Quincy Bragg, chief estimator Jay Smith, and office manager Loretta Halpin.

For 42 years Salinas Steel Builders has provided the Central Coast with consistently high-quality buildings that are done right, on time, and on budget. The company puts the dreams of Homer Goldman to work for its customers every day.

LAUREL INN

Though the Laurel Inn was actually ready for business on June 7, 1973, Tony and Al Sammut delayed opening their new Salinas hotel for two days. They did it so that their grand opening would fall on June 9, their mother's birthday.

"It was a very special day for all of us," says Tony Sammut. "We were a very poor family in Europe and in Detroit. When our parents saw us constructing a big building, putting up a restaurant—and they knew it was ours—we think it was the biggest event of their lives."

George and Antonia Sammut first immigrated to the United States from the island of Malta in the 1920s. During that time they worked and lived in Detroit, Michigan, where their first son, Joseph, was born. But the Great Depression forced the young family to leave the United States for Europe in 1930. They stayed abroad for several years but returned to this country, now with six children, in 1947.

Joseph, the oldest, was the first of the Sammut children to leave Detroit for sunnier climes. He arrived in California in 1958 and settled in Redwood City, taking a maintenance job at the Raychen Corporation. His brother, Charlie, soon followed, first opening a delicatessen, then founding the Bayline Paper Company.

In 1961 Al Sammut, lured by his brothers' stories of good weather and opportunity, packed up his wife and two children and headed for the Golden State. His first job in Redwood City, where he and his family settled, was as a machinist—the trade he had practiced in Detroit, with National O Ring.

Not long after Al settled in Redwood City he began talking to realtors about buying a motel. Though he had no real experience, Al had wanted to get into the hotel/motel business since long before moving to California.

But all of the available properties in the Bay Area were just too expensive for Al's startup budget. So when the realtor he was working with showed him the El Dorado Motel on North Main Street in Salinas, he didn't hesitate to put a down payment on the Sammut family's first motel venture.

Soon Tony Sammut followed his brothers to California, moving with his wife and three children to Redwood City in 1964. Like his younger brother, Al, Tony had been a machinist in Detroit, and soon found employment as a machinist/gear-cutter for Western Gear in Belmont.

In 1967 Tony joined Al as a partner in his motel venture. While Al ran the El Dorado in Salinas (he and his family actually resided at the motel), Tony continued to live and work in Redwood City.

The partnership was so successful that by 1971 Al and Tony began looking for another hotel to buy. After months of searching the Salinas Valley and nearby area, however, they couldn't find an existing facility they really liked. They decided, therefore, to build their own hotel this time.

Finding a site proved to be no easier than finding a building. The lot the two brothers eventually chose was picked only after they

The grand opening of Tony and Al Sammut's Laurel Inn in Salinas was delayed two days until the birthday of their mother, Antonia. Shown cutting the ribbon are (left to right): Al, Antonia, George, and Tony Sammut.

had spent many days standing on the Laurel Drive overpass counting the cars passing beneath their feet on Highway 101.

They knew a nearby vacant lot, situated on Laurel Drive just off the highway, that would be a perfect location for the working people, business managers, and sales reps who would be traveling through Salinas. It would give them room to build

a restaurant and a pool, as well as room to grow.

At first the lot's owner, well-known Salinas grower Gene Harden, wouldn't sell the Sammut brothers the small section of land they wanted for their hotel; he was planning to sell the entire parcel to a single developer. But when Harden's plans for a single sale fell through he agreed to subdivide his property and sell a portion of it to the Sammuts.

They built the 54-unit Laurel Inn and adjacent restaurant to start. Tony then moved his family to Salinas to run the new hotel (they also lived on the hotel property) while Al continued to manage the El Dorado.

Two years later they added the hotel's first wing of 28 rooms. Three years after that they purchased another section of Harden's property, converting it into another 26 rooms. By the time they were ready to add more rooms Harden had sold the rest of his lot. But the new owner was happy to sell the Sammuts what they needed, and the final addition was made

Above: Since the Sammuts first opened the 54-room hotel, they have made three additions for a total of 145 rooms.

Left: The Laurel Inn and Restaurant on Laurel Drive is conveniently located off Highway 101 for businesspeople traveling through Salinas.

in 1981 for a total of 145 rooms.

Al and Tony finally sold the El Dorado to their sister Madeline Borg and her husband, Joseph, who still run the motel. Another sister, Rita Gatt, who is Charlie Sammut's twin, also lives in Salinas.

Al and Tony Sammut have been business partners for more

than 20 years, and they say the success of that partnership, along with the participation of family members, is the reason for the success of their business. The brothers' hope is to see their hotel continue successfully in the hands of their children. Al's son, Alan, and Tony's daughter, Terry, are currently managing the Laurel Inn in Salinas, and Tony's son, George, is running the Sammut's newest venture, the Forest Park Inn in Gilroy.

As important as seeing the family business passing to their children is, nothing will compare to the day Al and Tony gave their mother her greatest birthday present. "For Al and me," says Tony, "nothing we've done since our grand opening has meant as much to us. It was the happiest day of our lives."

TYNAN LUMBER COMPANY

He's heard the story repeated by family members since he was a child, but Tynan Lumber Co. president Dirk Etienne doesn't seem to mind telling it one more time.

"It's an old story about my grandfather," he says. "He would be walking around the lumberyard and he would see a board lying on the ground. He'd stop then and there and ask the nearest workman what he thought the board was worth. The workman would answer that it was worth about a dollar, and my grandfather would say, 'Well, would you just leave a dollar lying on the ground?'

"I never thought it would happen, but I've caught myself saying the same thing."

Etienne represents the fourth generation of his family to manage the 77-year-old building supplies company. Founded in 1912 by his great-grandfather, Jan Tynan, the establish-

ment was Monterey County's first lumber company.

The elder Tynan first moved to Northern California from his home in Buffalo, New York, in the early 1900s to operate a hotel in San Francisco. He eventually migrated to Monterey where he was en-

For years Salinas Valley builders have relied upon Tynan Lumber Company for their lumber and building supplies. Founded in 1912 by Jan Tynan, the firm remains the oldest and most established lumber and building materials supplier in the area.

couraged by the Jack family (the famous cheese producers) to investigate local opportunities in the lumber business.

He soon established the Tynan Lumber Company, which he operated with the help of his son, L. Michael Tynan, from his first lumberyard in Monterey. The enterprise later expanded into Salinas, King City, Oakland, San Jose, and Paso Robles. Today the firm maintains its home office at the Salinas lumberyard, with branch operations in Monterey and King City.

During the 1920s the younger Tynan took over the family business, which also included a building and loan company. By 1982 he had built Tynan Building and Loan, eventually renamed Northern California Savings and Loan, into a firm with 63 branch offices and $1.9 billion in assets. When the com-

A flood in the winter of 1923 dampened business and spirits at Tynan Lumber, but the company made it through the rainy season undaunted.

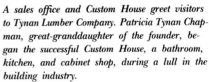

pany merged with Great Western Savings in 1982, Tynan was recognized for having served as chairman of the board of a company listed on the New York Stock Exchange longer than any other executive in history.

In 1980 Tynan invited his daughter, Patricia Tynan Chapman, to take over management of the family lumber business. Though she was a University of California, Berkeley, graduate, Patricia had little business experience, having spent most of her life as a full-time wife, mother, and homemaker.

"She was a middle-aged mom entering a male-dominated industry," says Etienne. "But that didn't stop

A sales office and Custom House greet visitors to Tynan Lumber Company. Patricia Tynan Chapman, great-granddaughter of the founder, began the successful Custom House, a bathroom, kitchen, and cabinet shop, during a lull in the building industry.

her. She came in here, felt her way through and breathed new life into this company."

Among Chapman's innovations was the addition to the Salinas operation of the Tynan Custom House, a custom bathroom, kitchen and cabinet shop that she opened shortly after she began managing the company. The opening of the cabinet shop was part of Chapman's strategy for coping with a lull in the building industry—a strategy that helped the firm weather some hard times.

Despite the construction slowdown of the early 1980s, Chapman continued to maintain her company's focus on the professional contractor. She avoided a trend that saw many of her competitors turning to the do-it-yourself market.

Today, with the fourth generation at the helm of the Salinas Valley's oldest and most respected building supply firm, Tynan Lumber Company carries on a tradition of service to professionals in the construction industry.

Delivery trucks keep lumber moving in and out of the Tynan resaw mill.

NOLAND, HAMERLY, ETIENNE & HOSS

Noland, Hamerly, Etienne & Hoss was founded in 1936 by attorney Harry L. Noland, who was raised on a cattle ranch in Colorado, graduated from Stanford Law School in 1928, arrived in Salinas shortly thereafter, and served as the youngest district attorney in California, occupying that position until 1935.

Noland incorporated the first produce companies to refrigerate lettuce. At 85, as the oldest practicing attorney in Monterey County, he comes to the office regularly and continues to advise clients.

The following attorneys have joined the firm:

Stanley Lawson joined the firm in 1946 and became a superior court judge in 1955.

Paul Hamerly, a graduate of Stanford University, specializes in corporations, estate planning, and probate. He is past trustee of the Salinas Union high School District and past president of the Monterey County Bar Association.

Myron "Doc" Etienne, a graduate of Hastings College of Law and trustee of that law school, specializes in land development, civil litigation, and general business law. He is a past president of the California Rodeo Association, a director of the Monterey Jazz Festival, and Fellow of the American Bar Association.

Peter T. Hoss, a native of Yosemite National Park and graduate of Stanford Law School, specializes in construction law, civil litigation, and general business, and is a past president of the Monterey County Bar Association.

James D. Schwefel, Jr., a graduate of Boalt Hall (U.C. Berkeley), emphasizes real estate, agricultural law, labor matters, and general business in his practice. He is a past president of Hartnell Board of Trustees and California Young Lawyers Association, and currently serves as

Throughout Monterey County the attorneys of Noland, Hamerly, Etienne & Hoss can be found serving a diverse roster of clients including individuals as well as the industries of agribusiness, development, finance, and retail.

president of the National Council of Alcoholism for Monterey County, Inc.

Martin J. May, a graduate of the University of San Francisco, specializes in taxation, corporation, and estate planning. He is a Certified Public Accountant, a former Internal Revenue agent, estate and gift tax examiner, and appellate conferee.

Stephen W. Pearson, a graduate of Hastings College of Law, specializes in civil litigation, commercial law, and general business law. He is a past president of the Monterey County Bar Association and director of Monterey College of Law.

Lloyd W. Lowrey, Jr., a graduate of Stanford University, specializes in administrative law, water law, and general business. He has served on the Hartnell College Board of Trustees and the Salinas Water Advisory Commission.

Anne K. Secker, a graduate of the University of Illinois, specializes in business litigation and commercial law. She is a director of the Monterey County Legal Services Corporation.

Paula Robinson, a graduate of Monterey College of Law, specializes in employment and civil litigation. She is a past president of Monterey County Young Lawyers

Association, serves on Hospice Development Committee, and is a director of Family Resource Center.

Anthony L. Lombardo, a graduate of the University of Santa Clara Law School, specializes in real estate matters, including use, zoning, and civil litigation. He is a member of the board of directors of the Monterey County Sheriffs Advisory Council and a member of the board of trustees of the York School.

Jerome F. Politzer, a graduate of the University of San Francisco Law School and also a certified public accountant, specializes in taxation and teaches graduate taxation and estate planning at Golden Gate University. He is treasurer of the Monterey County Young Lawyers Association.

Associates of the firm are Michael Masuda, Ralph P. Guenther, Mimi Matsumune, and Chris Gianascol.

In addition to attorneys, the firm employs a staff of 27 as secretaries, legal assistants, word processors, accounting, personnel, and support services.

Today the firm's broad countywide list of clients includes agribusiness clients, such as Mann Packing Co. and Sea Mist Farms, the Salinas Board of Realtors, banks such as First Interstate and Household Finance, as well as general and specialty contractors, retail businesses, and individual clients. The firm has been involved in such developments as Carmel Valley Golf & Country Club, Carmel Valley Ranch, Ventana Big Sur, Monterey Dunes Colony, as well as other real estate developments throughout the county.

Noland, Hamerly, Etienne & Hoss strives to provide quality legal services to the business community and individuals residing in Monterey County from its wide background of experience.

NESTLÉ FOODS, INC.

Chocolate is hardly the product one would normally associate with the nation's salad bowl. Yet, the Nestlé Foods plant in Salinas each week produces one million pounds of Crunch Bars, Toll House Morsels, Quik Chocolate Powder, chocolate coatings, and chocolate ice cream bar coatings.

The history of Nestlé Foods, Inc., in Salinas really begins in Switzerland more than 100 years ago when Henri Nestlé, a Swiss chemist who perfected the process for condensing milk, teamed with Daniel Peter, whose family perfected the process of making solid dark chocolate. In 1875 these two men, following Henri Nestlé's special recipe, created what is now the world's most popular confection—milk chocolate.

Nestlé's first American plant was built in Fulton, New York. That plant, which today is Nestlé's largest chocolate factory, installed its first chocolate production lines in 1907. Nestlé has been making milk chocolate in Salinas for 27 years and in Burlington, Wisconsin, for 22 years.

Joe Ramirez checks the Quik packaging line in the Salinas Nestlé Foods plant. Ramirez is one of many Nestlé employees who have been with the company for more than 25 years.

Why Salinas?

In the late 1950s Nestlé wanted to build a new plant to service its growing western market. The Salinas Valley's strategic location between the two major metropolitan areas of San Francisco and Los Angeles, its ideal weather, available labor force, excellent access to rail and major highways, and readily available supplies of sugar and fresh milk all made the Salinas site an ideal location.

"Nestlé makes the very best—chocolate" is among the most recognizable phrases in the confection industry. That phrase sums up a reputation earned through innovation, a single-minded dedication to quality, and a commitment to growth that over the decades has allowed Nestlé Food's Swiss parent, Nestlé S.A.,

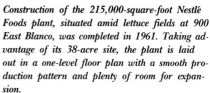

Construction of the 215,000-square-foot Nestlé Foods plant, situated amid lettuce fields at 900 East Blanco, was completed in 1961. Taking advantage of its 38-acre site, the plant is laid out in a one-level floor plan with a smooth production pattern and plenty of room for expansion.

to become one of the largest food and beverage companies in the world.

The company now distributes branded products on all five continents manufactured in 59 countries. This wide geographical spread contributes to economic growth by providing outlets for raw material producers along with jobs and professional training. In 1987 worldwide employment approached 163,000 people, and total sales exceeded $23 billion. Nestlé's sales growth in the United States comes from such well-known brands as Nescafe, Taster's Choice, Hills Brothers, Nestea, Carnation, Maggi, Crosse & Blackwell, Kerns, Stouffer's, Beech-Nut, MJB, and, of course, such well-known chocolate items as Toll House Morsels, Quik, Crunch, Alpine White, O'Henry, 100 Grand, Raisinets, Goobers, and Chunky.

The Nestlé Foods Salinas factory produces Nestlé Crunch, Quik, and Toll House Morsels, and has remained a major contributing member of the larger Nestlé family for more than 27 years.

Patrons

The following individuals, companies, and organizations have made a valuable commitment to the quality of this publication. Windsor Publications and the Salinas Area Chamber of Commerce gratefully acknowledge their participation in *The Salinas Valley: An Illustrated History*.

Arrow Lettuce Company*
Ausonio Construction Inc.*
Bank of Salinas*
Jim Bardin Ranch*
Belli* Christensen, AIA, Architects*
Bud of California*
The Castroville Artichoke People*
City of Salinas*
D'Arrigo Bros. Company*
First National Bank of Monterey County*
Fresh International*
Fresh Western Marketing, Inc.*
Golden West Restaurants*
Hartnell College*
Jerome Kasavan Associates, Inc.*
Lacey Automotive Parts Company*
The Lantis Corporation*
Laurel Inn*
McCormick & Company
   McCormick-Schilling Division*

Mann Packing Company*
Mill Construction Company*
Mills Distributing Company*
Nestlé Foods, Inc.*
Noland, Hamerly, Etienne & Hoss*
The Nunes Company, Inc.*
Pacific Bell
Pacific Gas & Electric Company*
Piini Realty*
John Pryor Company*
The Salinas Californian*
Salinas Steel Builders*
Salinas Valley Memorial Hospital*
Salinas Valley Wax Paper Company*
Scarr Moving & Storage, Inc.
John Snow Seed Company*
Steinbeck Federal Credit Union*
Stewart's Housewares & Gifts
Stone Container Corporation*
Struve and Laporte Funeral Chapel
Tanimura and Antle*
Tynan Lumber Company*

*Partners in Progress of *The Salinas Valley: An Illustrated History*. The histories of these companies and organizations appear in Chapter Eight, beginning on page 136.

Bibliography

Allen, Rutillus Harrison. "Economic History of Agriculture in Monterey County, California, During the American Period." Unpublished Ph.D. thesis. University of California, Berkeley, 1934.

Arden, Harvey. "East of Eden: California's Mid-coast." *National Geographic,* April 1984.

Armstrong, J. *Early History of the United Presbyterian Church of Salinas.* Salinas: Presbyterian Church, 1934.

Astro, Richard. "Steinbeck In Our Time." *Monterey Life,* July 1987.

Bancroft, Hubert Howe. *History of California* (7 vols.). San Francisco: The History Company, 1886.

Beck, Warren A., and Ynez D Haase. *Historical Atlas of California.* Norman: University of Oklahoma Press, 1974.

Becker, Robert H. *Disenos of California Ranchos.* San Francisco: The Book Club of California, 1964.

Bertano, David E., and Eduardo M. Diaz. "El Portuguese—Don Antonio Rocha, California's First Portuguese Sailor." *California History,* LXVI (September 1987), 188-195.

Blumann, Ethel, and Mabel W. Thomas, eds. *California Local History, A Centennial Bibliography.* Stanford: Stanford University Press, 1950.

Bolton, Herbert Eugene. *Anza's California Expeditions.* Berkeley: U.C. Press, 1930.

——————. *Diary of Pedro Fages.* Berkeley: U.C. Press, 1911.

——————. *Spanish Exploration in the Southwest, 1542-1706.* New York: Harper, 1916.

Brusa, B.W. *The Salinan Indians of California and Their Neighbors.* Berkeley: Naturegraph, 1975.

Bryant, Edwin. *What I Saw in California.* New York: A.S. Barnes and Co., 1850.

Clark, William B. *Gold Districts of California.* Sacramento: State of California, Division of Mines and Geology, 1963.

Colton, Walter. *Three Years in California.* New York: A.S. Barnes and Co., 1850.

Cook, Sherburne F. *The Conflict Be-tween the California Indian and White Civilization.* Berkeley: U.C. Press, 1976.

Cowan, Robert Ernest. *Bibliography of the History of California and the Pacific West, 1510-1906.* San Francisco: Book Club of California, 1914.

Coy, Owen C. *California County Boundaries.* Berkeley: California Historical Survey Commission, 1923.

——————. *Guide to the County Archives of California.* Sacramento: State of California, Historical Survey Commission, 1919.

Crouch, Steve. *Steinbeck Country.* New York: Crown Publishers, 1985.

Dakin, Susanna Bryant. *The Lives of William Hartnell.* Stanford: Stanford University Press, 1949.

Davis, William Heath. *Seventy-five Years in California.* San Francisco: John Howell, 1929.

Delmatier, Royce D.; Clarence F. McIntosh; and Earl G. Waters. *The Rumble of California Politics, 1848-1970.* New York: John Wiley and Sons, 1970.

DeNevi, Don, and Noel Francis Moholy. *Junipero Serra.* San Francisco: Harper and Row, 1985.

DeWitt, Howard. *Violence in the Fields.* Saratoga, Calif.: Century Twenty-One Publishing, 1980.

Dunn, Arthur. *Monterey County, California, California Land for Wealth, California Fruit for Health.* San Francisco: Sunset Magazine Homeseekers' Bureau, 1915.

Early, Thomas J. *Padres and People of Salinas.* Fresno: Academy Library Guild, 1953.

Eldredge, Zoeth S. *The March of Portola and the Discovery of the Bay of San Francisco.* San Francisco: The California Promotion Committee, 1909.

Engelhardt, Zephyrin. *San Antonio de Padua, The Mission in the Sierras.* Santa Barbara: Mission Santa Barbara, 1929.

Fages, Pedro. *A Historical, Political, and Natural Description of California.* Berkeley: U.C. Press, 1937.

Farquahar, Francis P., ed. *Up and Down California in 1860-1864. The Journal of William H. Brewer.* Berkeley: U.C. Press, 1966.

Fisher, Anne. *The Salinas, Upside-down River.* New York: Toronto, Farrar and Rinehard, 1945.

Galarza, Ernesto. *Farm Workers and Agribusiness in California, 1947-1960.* Notre Dame, Indiana: University of Notre Dame Press, 1977.

Garner, Robert William. *Letters From California, 1846-1847.* Edited by Donald Munroe Craig. Berkeley: U.C. Press, 1970.

Glass, Judith Chanin. "Conditions Which Facilitate Unionization of Agricultural Workers: A Case Study of the Salinas Valley Lettuce Industry." Unpublished Ph.D. thesis. University of California, Los Angeles, 1966.

Gordon, Burton L. *Monterey Bay Area: Natural History and Cultural Imprints.* Pacific Grove, CA.: Boxwood Press, 1974.

Griffin, Paul F., and C. Langden White. "Lettuce Industry of the Salinas Valley." *Scientific Monthly,* August 1955, pp. 77-84.

Guinn, James Miller. *History and Biographic Record of Monterey and San Benito Counties.* Los Angeles: Historic Record Co., 1910.

[——————.] *History of Monterey County, California.* San Francisco: Elliot & Moore, 1881.

——————. *History of the State of California and Biographic Record of Santa Cruz, San Benito, Monterey and San Luis Obispo Counties.* Chicago: Chapman Publishing, 1903.

Hammond, George Peter, ed. *Noticias de California.* San Francisco: Book Club of California, 1958.

Hannah, Shirley Harriet. "Early Development of the Salinas Valley." Unpublished M.A. thesis. Berkeley: University of California, Berkeley, 1936.

Harrison, E.S. *Monterey County.* Harrison's Series of Pacific Coast Pamphlets #3, Salinas, California. San Francisco: Pacific Press, 1889.

Heizer, Robert F., ed. *California Indians.* Vol. VIII of the *Handbook of North American Indians.* Edited by William C. Sturtevant. 20 vols. Washington, D.C.: Smithsonian Institution, 1978.

Heizer, Robert F., and M.A. Whipple.

The California Indians. Berkeley: U.C. Press, 1951.

Heizer, Robert F., ed. *The Costanoan Indians.* Cupertino, Calif.: California History Center, 1974.

Hittell, John S. *Hittell's Hand-Book of Pacific Coast Travel.* San Francisco: A.L. Bancroft and Co., 1895.

Hittell, Theodore H. *History of California.* San Francisco: Pacific Press Publishing House, 1885.

Hoadley, Walter E. "A Study of 170 Self-resettled Agricultural Families, Monterey County, California, 1939." Berkeley: By the author, 1940.

Hoffman, Ogden. *Reports of Land Cases . . .* San Francisco: Hubert, 1862.

Hoover, Mildred Brooke; Hero Eugene Rensch; and Ethel Grace Rensch. *Historic Spots in California.* Stanford: Stanford University Press, 1966.

Houston, James D. *Californians.* Berkeley: Creative Arts Books Co., 1985.

Howard, Donald M. *Lost Adobes of Monterey County.* Carmel, Calif.: Monterey County Archaeological Society, 1973.

—————. *Ranchos of Monterey County.* Carmel, Calif.: Antiquities Research Publications, 1978.

Jackson, Helen Hunt. *Glimpses of California and the Missions.* Boston: Little, Brown and Co., 1902.

Johnston, Robert B. *The Place Called La Natividad.* Salinas: By the author, 1985.

—————. *Salinas, 1875-1950, From Village to City.* Salinas: Fidelity Savings and Loan, 1980.

Jones, W.O. "A California Case Study in Location Theory: The Globe Artichoke on the Moro Cojo." *Journal of Farm Economics,* XXXI (1949).

Jones, William O. "The Salinas Valley: Its Agricultural Development, 1920-1940." Unpublished Ph.D. thesis. Stanford: Stanford University, 1947.

King, John Michael. "Historic Overview of the Elkhorn Slough Area." Unpublished report presented to the Department of Fish and Game, 1962.

King City, California, The First Hundred Years. King City: The San Antonio Valley Historical Association, 1986.

Kroeber, A.L. *Handbook of the Indians of California.* New York: Dover Publications, 1976.

Loomis, Noel M. *Wells Fargo.* New York: Clarkson Potter, Inc., 1968.

Lydon, Sandy. *Chinese Gold.* Capitola,

Calif.: Capitola Book Co., 1985.

March, Ray A. "Salinas' Son." *Monterey Life,* July 1987.

Margolin, Malcolm. *The Ohlone Way.* Berkeley: Heyday Books, 1978.

Marinacci, Barbara, and Rudy Marinacci. *California's Spanish Place-Names.* San Rafael, Calif.: Presidio Press, 1980.

Mason, J. *The Ethnology of the Salinan Indian.* Berkeley: U.C. Press, 1912.

Matthiessen, Peter. *Sal Si Puedes: Cesar Chavez and the New American Revolution.* New York: Random House, 1969.

McCarthy, Paul. *John Steinbeck.* New York: Frederick Unger Publishing Co., 1980.

McWilliams, Carey. *Factories In The Field.* Santa Barbara: Peregrine Publishers, 1971.

Messner, Mike. *Steinbeck Country in Dubious Homage.* Salinas: By the author, 1979.

Monterey County Archives. Monterey, Calif.: Bancroft Library, 1954.

Palou, Fray Francisco. *Historical Memoirs of New California.* Edited by Herbert E. Bolton. Berkeley: U.C. Press, 1926.

Pitt, Leonard. *The Decline of the Californios.* Berkeley: U.C. Press, 1970.

Pratt, Julius W. *Expansionists of 1898.* Baltimore: The Johns Hopkins Press, 1936.

Raup, H.F. "The Italian-Swiss in California." *California Historical Society Quarterly,* XXX (December 1951).

Reid, Robert Morrison. "Route of the Portola Expedition, 1769." Unpublished paper, n.d.

Reinstedt, Randall A. *Monterey's Mother Lode.* Carmel, Calif.: Ghost Town Publications, 1977.

—————. *Tales, Treasures and Pirates of Old Monterey.* Carmel, Calif.: Ghost Town Publications, 1976.

State of California, Disaster Office. *The Big Flood: California, 1955.* Sacramento: State Printing Office, 1956.

Steinbeck, John. "Always Something to do in Salinas." *Holiday,* June 1955.

—————. *In Dubious Battle.* New York: The Viking Press, 1938.

—————. *Of Mice and Men.* New York: The Viking Press, 1938.

—————. *The Grapes of Wrath.* New York: The Viking Press, 1939.

—————. "The Summer Before." *Monterey Life,* July 1987.

—————. *Their Blood Is Strong.* San Francisco: The Lubin Society, 1938.

Storer, Tracy I., and Lloyd P. Tevis, Jr. *California Grizzly.* Lincoln: University of Nebraska Press, 1978.

"Survey of Attitudes of Salinas Citizens Toward Japanese-Americans During W.W.II." Salinas: Salinas Chamber of Commerce, n.d.

Taylor, Ronald B. *Chavez and The Farm Workers.* Boston: Beacon Press, 1975.

U.S. Congress. House Select Committee Investigating National Defense Migration. *National Defense Migration: Fourth Interim Report.* H.R. 2124, 77th Congress, 2nd Session, May 1942.

U.S. National Park Service. "The History of Wildland Fires In the Gabilan Mountains Region of Central Coast California." A report by Jason Greenlee and Andrew Moldenke. Pinnacles National Monument, unpublished report, 1982.

U.S. Works Progress Administration. *Historical Episodes in Monterey County, 1542-1905.* Monterey, Calif.: WPA, 1938.

Valle, Rosemary K. "James Ohio Pattie and the 1927-28 Alta California Measles Epidemic." *California Historical Quarterly,* LII (Spring 1973).

Verardo, Jennie. "A Short History of the Castroville Artichoke Festival." *Castroville Artichoke Festival.* Marina, Calif.: Castroville Artichoke Festival Committee, 1987.

Watkins, Rolin G. *History of Monterey and Santa Cruz Counties, California.* 2 Vols. Chicago: S.J. Clarke Publishing Co., 1925.

Wells, Andrew J. "Monterey County." *Sunset,* July 1911.

Woolf, Paul Nicholas. "A Historical Appraisal of the Flour-milling Industry in California." Unpublished Ph.D. thesis. University of California, Los Angeles, 1939.

Woolfenden, John, and Amelie Elkinton. *Cooper.* Pacific Grove, Calif.: The Boxwood Press, 1983.

Newspaper Sources
Castroville Times
Gonzales Tribune
Monterey Peninsula Herald
Salinas Daily Index
Salinas Daily Journal
Salinas Index-Journal
Salinas Californian
San Francisco Call
San Francisco Chronicle

Index